Jewish Tales Untold

Jewish Tales Untold

A 21st century Jewish regard for facts and fantasies

Ray Kohn

Ray Kohn

CONTENTS

CONTENTS

CONTENTS

CONTENTS

PREFACE

Jewish Tales Untold

Jewish Tales Untold gives you three books in one. The first has celebrated Biblical personalities telling us what really happened, what they did and thought. They include Noah and his family, Cain and Abel, Abraham and Isaac, Jacob's extensive family, Moses, Samson, David and Goliath, the angel Gabriel, Daniel, and the brothers Shadrach, Meshach, and Abednego, true Christian pilgrims, the Devil, God and the seraphim. You meet them all and are invited to see the Bible in a new light – more human, more realistic, more relevant to our everyday lives.

The second is a fantastic set of tales that reveal the hopes and fears that all of us share in imaginative accounts through sci-fi, comedy and myth. In this book we visit far-off planets with very familiar issues, astonishing angels and some who are not at all angelic, beautiful but deadly royalty, the wealthiest man on Earth, a phenomenal chef, Buddha, a recollection of ancient myths and imaginary and not-so-imaginary wars. This book contains much Jewish good humour as well as some serious subjects.

In the third we meet the enigmatic tzadik – a Jewish sage – who describes the Universe in which we live, and the issues that confront us all once we question what we are told. Conversations cover time and relativity, Plato and philosophy, music and creativity, politics and heroes, choice and free will, and the significance of the Shabbos candle. This book addresses the experiences that we think are happening and our hopes for the future.

But to give a flavour of what the author regards as the basic tenets of writing: he presents us first with a bunch of roses.

A BUNCH OF ROSES

My rabbi teaches a popular writing course. He asserts: "Every story must have a beginning, a middle and an end. The opening introduces characters and some form of conflict. The central section develops the characters and brings the conflict to a head. Finally, the conflicts are resolved one way or another. Novels, plays, short stories – they all obey this rule. Wuthering Heights, Othello, the tales of Guy De Maupassant, Saul Bellow; everywhere you see the same structure.

Listen to me! If a text fails to conform to this formula, then it is not a story!"

My rabbi was absolutely firm in his instruction. Obey the rule or fail as a storyteller was his constant message. I remember the first time I met one of his other apprentices, a charming woman clothed in the most expensive fashion and made up in stark black and red colours to look like a slightly surreal baby doll. She put her great success in having her stories published down to always keeping and never deviating from the rabbi's rules. She explained to me that my abject failure to take the publishing industry by storm was due to my fascination in trying out different structures that were bound to fall flat.

"Why can't a story be like a bunch of roses?" I asked the rabbi. "Just a beautiful gesture without a past and future."

He shook his head. I had seen him do this when faced with a particularly incompetent amateur writer.

"Listen," he said patiently. "Even a bunch of roses has a past: they were planted and grew. Then they were formed into a presentable bunch. And finally, they wither and die."

I had to agree with this analysis but pressed on regardless. "Surely when I hand this bunch to a friend or hostess at a party, it has no past and future, its meaning is simply defined by the present context?"

Impatiently he replied. "Please yourself. All I am telling you is that if you persist in this ridiculous pursuit of some perverse attempt at a story, you will end up with a text that is completely meaningless. No one will want to read it, and you will only see the error of your ways when it is too late to develop your potential as a true storyteller."

And maybe he was right. At his funeral yesterday, attended by about five hundred people, the address was delivered by the same charming, fashionably dressed woman. She gave an emotional performance during which she described her reputation as a best-selling writer due to her adherence to the precepts of the teacher.

"He knew that success could only be achieved by an understanding of, and deference to, the one true way, the discipline at the heart of storytelling, at the heart of living life itself."

As she spoke, I looked around and saw other authors sitting in rows, davening vigorously and in unison or nodding in agreement to her words. They too had understood and deferred to the way of the master.

By contrast, my experimentation led me to attempt many alternatives to the golden rule. I wrote letters and poems. I trifled with multimedia presentations and even developed a series of minimalist musical compositions. I explored sculpting and painting but gave up when my poor technical skill and abject lack of talent became obvious even to me. Eventually, as a final ironic form of capitulation and just before our wedding, I sent the charming lady a bunch of roses.

2

BOOK ONE: OLD JEWISH TALES

3

TERAH'S ORATION

My beloved family,

We are gathered to mourn the loss of your brother, my son, Haran. Like so many over this year in Ur, he was struck down by the epidemic that has spread from the Euphrates and shows little sign of abating. You know he was brave, helping families who had lost children to the fever, before catching the illness himself. He leaves his son, Lot, and daughters, Milcah and Iscah. And they, like you my surviving children, ask what we should do next.

To find the future, we should examine our past. How did we come to be in Ur? Who brought us here all those years ago? You all know it was the wisest of our ancestors, Atrahasis.

Why did he bring his family to Ur? He lived in the cultured city of Shuruppak and was the trusted advisor to King Ziusudra. Sumerian leaders of that era encouraged exploration and scientific investigation and Atrahasis was given permission to leave the freshwater lakeside of his home to take three ships on an expedition to gather flora and fauna along the far-flung shores of the Mediterranean. He left with his family and some of the city's best scientists. The expedition was a great success, and they gathered a vast collection that filled the accompanying cargo ships with rare plants and unusual animals. But after three years, Atrahasis returned to discover that his home city had disappeared beneath the great flood when the Mediterranean had burst through the silt and shells that held the sea back from their lake.

Atrahasis was devastated. The great flood had destroyed the city and all those whom he had known, including Ziusudra, the last of the Sumerian kings. Instead, he found himself landing on the strange shores of the Black Sea and the newly emerged Akkadian empire. King Sargon let it be known that he intended building a new city, Akkad, to which he expected Atrahasis to appear with his prize collections. However, Atrahasis was shrewd and did not expect the same level of support from Sargon as he had enjoyed from Ziusudra. So, he sought a better option which would also afford himself and his family greater safety.

Sargon had made his daughter, Enheduanna, the High Priest of the Moon God, in Ur. Atrahasis loaded his precious collection onto wagons and headed south as he knew that Ur was more like the city where he had been born rather than the yet-to-be-built city of Akkad. On arrival, he was confronted by sentries demanding to know if he recognized the primacy of the Moon God – Inanna in Sumerian, or No-on in Akkadian. As a refugee, he knew better than to reject the Akkadian name give him by the guards, No-ah, and he led his entourage into the city, dedicating the zoo he founded to Enheduanna.

So, what do we learn from Noah? He was forced to find a new home for himself, and his family and we now find ourselves in a similar situation. It is not safe for us to remain in Ur so we must, like Noah, assess our best options as to where we should go.

Here is what I believe we should do. We cannot know the future, but we can spread our options by having family members move to different locations. Then, if one finds an excellent place to live whereas another discovers that they have landed in an area that is unsafe, they can come together again in the safe place.

Nahor, it is your responsibility to take your family up the Euphrates to settle in the plains to the north. Milcah, having lost her father Haran, should accompany you and be your wife.

Lot, you are now the head of your family and should travel to Jordan where there are already established cities as well as a fertile plain. You and your wife may explore the rural life offered in the fields or the urban life offered in the city of Sodom. The main danger you may face is being caught out in the sun as the plains offer no shade or protection. We have heard tales of men and women exposed without shade or water being found next day as dried-out husks. So, beware!

Sarah, all the family recognize you as the cleverest and most educated of us all. Yet you remain humble and without the pretensions of some who remain as besotted Moon god worshippers. You need protection as you travel to Canaan with your brother Abraham: so, he must pretend to be your husband.

Today, we say farewell to our beloved son, Haran. Tomorrow, like Noah before us, we must set off so that our family can survive and thrive.

4

BROTHERHOOD

"I don't understand," he admitted to his brother.

"Don't worry," came the response, "it will all become clear tonight."

That evening, he was to be entered into the Ancient Brotherhood. Nobody knew how far back the Brotherhood went, but its initiation ceremony was full of bizarre rituals that only seemed to make sense to initiates.

"Do we have a leader?" he asked his brother.

"No, not really. Normally, one Brother stands out in the fraternity and is recognized."

"Do we have elections?"

"No, not in living memory."

"Shall I be given a secret name?"

"Stop asking questions. You were like this at Bar Mitzvah classes, but I'm no rabbi. The ceremony will explain itself."

His brother was short with him, but this was understandable. He was a busy man, with many people coming and going to do business with him. But now he was going to introduce him into the secrets of initiation, so his questions would be answered. He imagined a Society dedicated to Liberty, Equality, Fraternity: but knew that the Brotherhood was a lot older than the 18th century. He puzzled his way back through all the brothers in history and ended up thinking of himself as a dreaming Joseph guiding the Brotherhood, and the World, through seven years of famine with his prophetic insights. He enjoyed these daydreams but was cut short by his brother telling him to get ready to leave.

The hall was darkened so you could not see the walls from the candle-lit circle of chairs in the center. Men guarded the doors, and an armed escort accompanied the brothers to their places. He was not permitted to sit but stood by a small table in the middle of the circle. He was aware of the many members of the Society taking their places but could not watch them because of the blindfold. He waited, impatiently. Eventually, his own brother called out and the handkerchief was removed from his eyes.

"Look down on the table and read the oath" It was very long and involved swearing eternal allegiance to the fraternal faith, submission to the will of the Ancient Brotherhood, life-long love for the friends he would make here, and the tearing of some of his clothes. Nearing the end of his reading, the guard beside him silently placed a capsule upon the table.

"Swallow the pill!" All the men began to hum. It started very low and quiet, but gradually grew into a many-layered chant whose intensity increased until he felt that it was bursting from within his head. He started to hallucinate.

"Now see yourself. Who are you?" The Brotherhood had started to chant words, but he could not focus on what they were. Pictures and time rolled before him as he realized what they were saying.

"What is your name? What is your name? What is your name?" Suddenly he seized the automatic pistol from his startled guard and shot his brother through the head.

"I am Cain," he cried. There was total silence in the hall as his brother's body rolled to the floor. He stepped over it and took his seat as the Brotherhood started to applaud.

5

ASENATH'S TESTIMONY

I write this testimony for my sons, Ephraim and Manasseh. You will read this and know the truth. But it is for you to decide whether to wisely ignore it or cast yourselves into an unknown future outside the benefits of whatever inheritance you may receive from my grandfather, Jacob.

You know that Jacob had only one daughter, Dinah. Her great love was the handsome Hivite Prince, Shechem. Dinah's brothers disapproved of what they regarded as an infatuation with a man who had not undergone the circumcision introduced as an essential health protection by the brilliant Sarah, daughter of Terah of Ur. But he agreed to have the operation as he was equally in love with Dinah and would do anything to be allowed to marry her. She was already pregnant with her daughter – that's me, your mother. But instead of allowing them to live peacefully together, her vile brothers Simeon and Levi, came with knives to carry out the circumcision and, instead, murdered my father.

I believe that my mother, Dinah, has ever since then regarded her brothers as little better than animals. They put it about that my birth was the result of Shechem raping her. Nothing could be further from the truth. But, unlike me, they are not interested in the truth. The twelve sons of Jacob are a peculiar collection: some are appalling human beings whilst others are pleasantly normal. Ever since the times of Sarah when she questioned the wisdom of bearing children from partners who were closely related, a question hangs over whether these close relationships bring forth children damaged from birth. Are they responsible for their actions or are they already so damaged as to be beyond the reach of civilized action? Some may, of course, be abnormal in ways that are of benefit – but they are the exception.

Jacob had seven children by his sister, Leah. Issacher is unusually clever – a scholar and gentleman. The "normal two" are my mother Dinah (damaged by her evil brothers) and Zebulon, who fled the awful family to spend most of his life at sea. The other four, Reuben, Simeon, Levi and Judah, are the most dreadful men you are ever likely to meet. All four hated their "weird brother", Joseph, and after setting him down a well, pulled him out to sell to passing slavers! How could anyone justify these actions? Reuben decided he wanted to have sex with his father's bed companion, Bilhah. So, her two children, Dan and Naphtali, may or may not be Jacob's children – perhaps he only has ten sons. How will we ever know? Judah is immensely strong and has a towering temper. In one tantrum he murdered Jashub, the king of Tappuah. And never forget, Simeon and Levi murdered your grandfather. Jacob's two sons by his servant, Zilpah, are lovely, normal human beings. Gad and Asher – just like Dan and Naphtali – are totally unlike Reuben, Simeon, Levi and Judah. Please bear this in mind, my lovely sons, when I speak about how I have behaved.

Jacob's two sons by his cousin, Rachel, are also strange. Benjamin is like a spoilt brat – even as an adult. He expects everyone to serve him. His brother Joseph is one of the strangest men in Egypt. He is almost completely incompetent in everyday activities. I sometime wonder whether he may have even fallen down that well and the brothers just decided to get rid of him when they found him. But he has an extraordinary capacity to work out the most complicated puzzles without a moment's thought. He is an idiot savant, able to calculate the precise requirements for silo storage of grain, the exact proportions of wagons needed to transport the precious food and the exact dimensions and length of pipework required to ensure a steady supply of water to the city. He is a genius and a bumbling idiot and Jacob ordered that he and I should be married.

You are my sons, and it may help you to pretend that Joseph is your father. But there is no way that I wanted to be married to my uncle or bear damaged children by him. You can observe his slight body and his sallow complexion whilst both of you are powerfully built, tall and have shining, black skin. The man whom I wanted to be with is tall and strong – just like you. He is Potiphar, the Captain of Pharoah's Guards and unlikely to feel threatened by any thoughts that Simeon and Levi might have towards him. His wife, Zuleika, is the most shameless tart keen and willing to sleep with almost anyone at court. So, it has not been difficult for your real father and mother to be together without interruption over the past years.

When you read my testimony, I recommend that you show it to nobody and go on to enjoy a happy and prosperous life. But at least you will be able to live in the knowledge of why you are both so strong and healthy.

6

THE BLUNDER

I witnessed an amusing scene today. Rebbe Simon was stopped in the street by a Chassidic couple. I know the couple. They are keen on researching family trees and claim that they can trace theirs back to Ruth and the Moabites. They are wonderful people who play as a husband-and-wife duet in local concerts. For them, playing music is communing with the divine. For them, Rebbe Simon is something of a renegade.

"Rebbe," the wife called, "why could you not come to our concert last night?"

"Good morning, Tara. I must apologize for missing it. I think I was drunk." Rebbe Simon has never been drunk in his life, but he enjoys teasing Tara's husband, Henry.

"You should not say such things!" He had succeeded in provoking Henry. There followed a mock apology by Rebbe Simon, with the promise that in future he would try to behave with more decorum in public. It was then that the Rebbe launched his sting in the tail or – as he would say – he "came to the point".

"Henry, I often seem to blunder about. But you should not always condemn such foolishness. After all, the Almighty committed many blunders and I have never heard you condemning God."

Tara and Henry looked at each other. They were obviously puzzled by this remark – upset, even. They knew that Rebbe Simon was a respected teacher with views that were occasionally offbeat. But he could always support them with logic and scholarship. Challenging him should be undertaken with some trepidation.   So, they started cautiously.

"Rebbe Simon:" this was Tara, "we feel uplifted by the splendors of God's Universe. We dwell upon the wonders of creation. Are you sure that the blemishes of which you speak are not simply those that we cause by our own inadequacy?"

"We are often inadequate in carrying out our side of the covenant," the Rebbe agreed; "but you know the Almighty has made mistakes in trying to work out His side of the deal." This was too much for Henry.

"You have just promised to behave better in public, and now you are denouncing the Almighty in the street!"

"Henry, do not get so worked up. I am only telling you what you have already read in the scriptures. Before God worked out His agreement with Abraham, He had a preliminary trial with Noah. What had not occurred to Him was that His side of the bargain did not require drowning everyone else. After the event, it is written that the Lord regretted His own behavior and said that He would not do anything like it again. What the Almighty realized, even if it was too late to save millions of living creatures, was that the dark side of human nature is carried in all of us. So, it cannot be destroyed by killing whole sections of the population since it lives on in the survivors."

"That is just your interpretation," said Tara.

"Of course," smiled Rebbe Simon; "but you can see where the idea of genocide started if you read the scriptures in this way."

"This is scandalous!" Henry started walking away with Tara. The crowd that had gathered started to make way

"Nonsense!" called Rebbe Simon. "If it's scandal you want, just remember where the Moabite family tree springs from." Tara and Henry stopped. The crowd was quiet. "My dear friends," Rebbe Simon continued. "You must know that the Moabites had a long and distinguished history before the time of Ruth. After the Flood, that was intended to wipe away sin, Abraham's nephew Lot fathered the first Moabite from an incestuous relationship with his daughters." Then, to save the musical Moabites further embarrassment, Rebbe Simon commended the crowd to read the scriptures more attentively and they would discover – as had the Almighty – that all our ancestry has its dark side.

7

THE SEMINAR

Every year, Rebbe Simon looked forward to the two-day open seminar. He would announce the theme six months in advance, and he usually received a couple of dozen applications straight away. By the time the seminar date arrived, he was having to limit admission as the rooms would not hold the numbers.

Simon understood the popularity of the seminar had little to do with him. Neither was fame nor fortune a factor for those who came. There were no prizes for best entries and no judges to decide on which winners should be published. Any suggestion of so vulgar a motivation would have distressed Simon for, although he was aware of this flaw to his personality, he could not suppress a streak of intellectual snobbery. However, this year was the same as every other - the only reason why the participants came was because they were all keen to hear each other: and were grateful that he organized the event which allowed this to happen. All of them had to submit a written contribution prior to the seminar: and Simon selected a few to be read out in the opening plenary. This year's subject was Abraham, Isaac, and the sacrifice.

To launch the proceedings, Simon read the passage in the Torah, in Hebrew and in English translation. Then he spoke briefly about the perspectives offered by some of the great commentators. And to end his contribution, he declaimed the famous poem by Wilfred Owen:

So Abram rose, and clave the wood, and went,
And took the fire with him, and a knife.
And as they sojourned both of them together,
Isaac the first-born spake and said, My Father,
Behold the preparations, fire and iron,
But where the lamb for this burnt-offering?
Then Abram bound the youth with belts and straps,
And builded parapets and trenches there,
and stretched forth the knife to slay his son.
When lo! an angel called out of heaven,
Saying, Lay not thy hand upon the lad,
Neither do anything to him. Behold,
A ram, caught in a thicket by its horns;
Offer the Ram of Pride instead of him.
But the old man would not so, but slew his son,-
And half the seed of Europe, one by one.

Then he called on the first writer, Rachel, to read her submission. She stood up but was too small to be visible to most in the hall. So, he called her out to the front where she looked a little embarrassed. But she soon lost her shyness as she started to read her contribution.

"I was lost. I had become separated from the others in an early morning mist on the mountainside. I climbed slowly - a zig-zag path that soon left the light cloud behind. As noon approached, I had to look for shelter from the sun. I looked down the slope: the mist had long since gone. The air trembled and I imagined that I could see my companions. But the mirage disappeared, and I felt lonely and anxious.

With the sun directly above, there was no shade behind rocks. However, a rough patch of vegetation clung to the sandy ridge I had reached. I crawled down into it, lay still, and watched for any sign of movement that could herald the arrival of my friends.

Later in the afternoon, I heard men's voices. The air had grown a little cooler; but was so still that I could not guess how far away they were. I thought that I would pick my way over to the edge where I could survey the slopes below and spot where they were. But when I tried to move, I discovered that brambles had caught in my coat. Every way I tried to turn seemed to entangle me further in the thicket.

Suddenly the voices were very close. I inclined my head to catch a glimpse of the strangers. With some relief, I realised that they had seen my predicament and were coming over to help. One of them hacked away at the branch whose thorns had barred my escape. I felt it give way; it was lifted clear and I walked free. With an identical movement, the man with cold eyes hacked at my throat whilst a young boy looked on. As I gave way, the child walked free."

The applause was restrained. Obviously, most of the audience were not as intrigued as Simon had been to think about the story from the perspective of the goat. Simon felt that he had to put his own gloss on Rachel's story. He started to talk about the symbolism of "rough and hairy" as opposed to those with smooth skin or smooth tongue. So, the sacrifice is either smooth Isaac or the goat. Then there is Jacob versus Esau (with Jacob using goatskin to win Isaac's blessing). Then there is smooth Joseph against his rough brothers (especially Levi). Joseph versus Levi in the second generation finds Moses, Aaron and Ephraim on one side versus Gershon, Kohath and Merari. The third generation is Joshua's fight with Korah – the open rebellion. Simon felt he was getting further into deep water; but instead of stopping, he went on: "In Egypt we even have the priesthood of Amun (whose symbol is the rough-skinned snake) against the first Egyptian monotheists, the followers of Aten, whose political leader was Tiye - a smooth-skinned woman..." Rachel interrupted. "I'm not sure that I meant any of that, Simon. If anything, the stuttering Moses as opposed to the smooth-talking Aaron might give us hope that the World does not have to be run only by smooth operators." Simon smiled. He knew that he had gone too far and was pleased by the mild rebuke. So, he called for the next speaker, old David.

David had the slightly restrained, shrunken appearance of a holocaust survivor. He had sad eyes that seemed to shield him from the looks of others. Incongruously, he spoke with a huge, booming voice and remained seated as he read his little piece.

" For a second in every millennium, there is a moment when God can intervene and, with an imperceptible touch, alter the history of the World. If He had not made the goat twitch, then Abraham would not have seen it. Isaac would have died, and the following 4000 years of Jewish suffering could have been avoided."

The nods amongst the knot of older people contrasted sharply with the shaking of heads from the group of young scholars with whom Rachel had returned to sit. Simon called the next contributor immediately. He was the well-known teacher - Leo Levine. He used his contribution as rough notes to which he only occasionally referred. As he took the discussion, Simon could not stop thinking of Leo as the smoothest man he knew.

Leo spoke first about whether Abraham had any intention of killing Isaac. Perhaps he wanted to seem to be prepared to carry out the act as a demonstration of the significance of anything he might define as God's will. For that reason, the goat would have had to be tethered beforehand. Perhaps Abraham was disingenuous but wanted to appear as an iron-willed leader to the tribe. So, what was the symbolic significance of the goat? One man in the audience answered: "Was it a sacrifice to Abraham's pride?" Another ventured: "Would the tether matter? The goat still symbolizes Isaac. We still have to be prepared to sacrifice everything we value if it is God's will." But Leo shook his head. There was a silence in the hall.

No-one seemed to be able to make that conceptual leap for which he was asking. Then Simon spoke. "Do any of you know the poem by Yeats called 'The Long-Legged Fly'?" Most of those present nodded. Simon went on: "You remember that it starts:

That civilisation may not sink,
its great battle lost,
quiet the dog, tether the pony
to a distant post;
our master Caesar is in the tent
where the maps are spread,
his eyes fixed upon nothing,
a hand under his head.
His mind moves upon silence.
Like a long-legged fly upon the stream

Well, perhaps the pony's tether is like Leo's goat's tether. It is the guarantee of civilization. It is what prevents the killing of the children, or – in Caesar's case – the overrunning of the Empire." Leo liked this, but then posed one further question. "What happens if Isaac sees the tether?"

A short murmur as people talked amongst themselves led to Rachel suggesting that, since Isaac never gave Abraham away, we should see him as starting to learn the tricks of the trade before becoming the leader himself. "You mean that the leadership is just a succession of crooks?" asked Simon. Someone else called out that perhaps Isaac was really naive and believed that God had actually tethered the goat. A few laughed at this: but no-one thought it was funny when old David said he thought that Isaac would have said nothing to have something on his father. "Or perhaps the whole thing never happened," David continued, "but was a brilliant invention by Isaac to legitimize his leadership later." Simon called a halt to Leo's free discussion. "I am pleased that you are beginning to think about the whole story from Isaac's point of view," Simon said. "The last contribution for this morning will be Moshe Joseph's."

The young man stood up. Although he was still only a student and unmarried, his hair was starting to thin. As he spoke, he never stopped looking around as if expecting an abrupt interruption that never arrived. He read with a nervous, staccato voice.

"Abraham, my father, is into head games. That is fine by me. He plays for high stakes, but I know I am smarter than he is. Today, at last, we are going to play for the leadership.

'For me to retain authority, you must die.' This is his opening card played in the guise of human sacrifice demanded by God.

'Change the deck.' This is my obvious counter by suggesting that we climb the mountain. After all, you do not want to be seen as a child-killer by the rest of the tribe.

'I adopt a low-risk/no-risk strategy,' he maneuvers himself into this position with sincerely felt protestations about carrying it out with a heavy heart.

'Here is a gambit.' This is a risky move by me. The gambit is feigned meek submission. But the alternatives are either open rebellion or guerrilla warfare. Unfortunately, he is twice as big as me and carries all the authority he needs in the tribe to make open rebellion a spectacular form of suicide. Guerrilla warfare (i.e. going along with his will but being picky and objectionable) would make his game harder for him. But it would only be working on his low-risk/no-risk move without in any way removing the certainty of him carrying through his primary objective.

So, he responds: 'I accept your gambit.' This is really a forced move. He can scarcely object to my submission to the will of God. But, of course, this is the opening for which I am waiting.

'Double or quits.' This is my raising of the stakes. I am confident that it will prove too rich for my father. When faced with certain defeat in one line of play, it is perfectly acceptable to propose rule changes to the games-master. What I am offering is double the return in the next generation if I am given the leadership now. Given the prospect of a tribe committed to delivering double the return in each succeeding generation, God is tempted. Of course, He knows that some generations will fail to make due payment. But, looking at the deal over millennia, God obviously decided that mine was a better offer than Abraham's."

8

BEAUTY AND BEAST

As a child, he was called monster. He did not know why he was so different from other young boys, but when he gazed at his own reflection, he could not fail to see the bulging forehead that fascinated passers-by. When he looked down from his unusual height, he was confronted by hands and feet whose enormous size made him feel that they were not part of him at all.

Home was an unhappy place. His father usually rolled in drunk and gave him a beating for no reason. When sober, he would recount again and again the same story of how as a young warrior he had bravely set out across the mountains and captured his bride from the neighboring tribe. His wedding had been a great event, and his daughter was the most beautiful girl in the village; but then he would lapse into silence. Occasionally he would lurch on in his story to the moment when his wife produced the monster whose sheer size had killed her in childbirth. More drink and a beating followed.

At school, he was shunned by other children. Girls ran away screaming "the monster is coming to get me!" Boys did not want to play with someone who was already taller than their teachers. The teachers did not know how to speak to a child who towered above them but whose mental development lagged so far behind everyone else. He would wander off alone with his own thoughts and, when no one was looking, shed more than a tear.

His father made him dig the hard ground around their home. There they grew a meagre crop of vegetables that his sister would make into a tasteless broth. After the meal, he would set off into the hills rather than wait for his father's regular descent into depression. Solitary walks high above the village brought both relief and pain: relief from the ignominy and ostracism meted out to him daily; and pain around his heart as he panted for breath whilst climbing the steep slopes. One evening, he caught the distant sound of singing coming from further up the mountainside. Curious, he decided to investigate and forced himself to overcome the pain of the ascent to discover the source. As he climbed, the sweet voice grew louder, and he could hear the plucking of a lyre. The music echoed around the rocks. He peeped through a crevice between two boulders and saw a young man surrounded by goats. He was singing to himself as he stroked the lyre. The goats ignored him, but the performance was magical. This was beautiful singing from a beautiful boy!

Carefully descending the mountain, he was glad that he

had not shown himself to so lovely a musician. He felt his appearance would have destroyed the bond that he imagined now existed between the singer and his invisible audience. Approaching home, he was puzzled by the appearance of two strangers coming out holding his sister between them. He shouted for them to leave her alone; but they were armed with staves and threatened him if he stood in their way. As they ran past him, he grabbed one by the head and pulled. The breaking neck made a sickening sound and the man fell to the ground. The other man let go of his captured bride and ran away. A moment later, his father still half asleep with drink, staggered out and demanded to know what all the fuss was about. Seeing the dead man, he demanded that his monstrous son bury the intruder before the vultures arrived. His sister glared at him and sullenly returned to the unhappy home.

Next day, his father was in angry mood. He denounced him as a killer: first of his mother and now of the brother of the man he had arranged for his sister to marry. He told him that there was no place for him in his house any longer. "It is time for you to learn to be a man," he shouted. Later that day a fat man arrived wearing an unfamiliar uniform. "I am the Recruiting Sergeant," he announced. "Come with me and meet your friends in arms." He followed him to the military camp where his friends turned out to be a rough gang of men. As they lined up to parade, the Sergeant called out their names. Each one answered but when it came to his turn, he was slow to respond. The Sergeant marched up to him. "Ah! We have a tough one here," he called to the others in the line. "Already killed a man before he has even been in a battle!

You think you are tough, don't you?" And before he could answer, the Sergeant punched him hard in the stomach. Bent double, he felt the Sergeant kick his legs from under him. As he crashed to the ground amid laughter from his so-called friends, he heard the Sergeant say, "here you will learn that you are nothing."

And so, it was. The Sergeant ensured that, on a daily basis, it was confirmed that he was nothing. He washed the latrines; cleaned the Sergeant's boots; learnt to march up and down without thinking; and was told to forget about the home he had left. He was taught to fight with a stave and, after receiving many cuts and bruises, discovered how to defend himself. And all the time, the other recruits regarded him as a freak. They were all twice as old as him, yet he was more than a head taller than any of them. They poked fun at him but, once he had learnt how to wield the stave, none challenged him. Finally, the Sergeant paid him the first compliment that he had ever received. "You could be a good soldier."

When war broke out, he was given a huge stave. The men marched out to the hills where they knew they would meet the enemy. The armies faced one another across the open, stony ground and the commanders shouted to one another. Both agreed that a full-scale battle would be foolish because deaths on both sides would result in loss of labor for the fields in the coming season and starvation for both communities. So, to everyone's relief it was agreed that each army would choose a champion who would fight, one-to-one, to decide who should be declared the victor.

Musing on his life, he wondered whether his sister had

found any happiness or whether she was now permanently in thrall to their awful father. He looked around and saw the cruel faces of his comrades, baying for blood but hoping that they would not be chosen to face the enemy champion. He peered across to the enemy and saw only a crowd of ragged men who, like them, had been sent to fight by an unseen leader. Suddenly, to his consternation, he felt the strong arm of the Sergeant across his back. "Time for you to fight," he said, and thrust him forward into the open space. He looked back and saw his comrades laughing and shrieking. "Go on, Goliath, kill him, kill him!" He looked across and saw the enemy champion walking forward with confidence. He swallowed hard as he saw that it was the beautiful singer wielding nothing more than a sling.

Gazing past the enemy and across the landscape, he thought he glimpsed how men would always fight and kill for ownership of this land. Yet he knew its stones and sand and hard ground were hardly worth dying for. Then he looked at the faces of the men on both sides, and it was as if a spirit of evil had been aroused and was sweeping through them. He was a giant, but he was still a child. In his innocence, he wondered whether the fight would be the occasion when all the evil would be released, and men would cease killing one another. Perhaps he could die in that cause: perhaps he could release them from their terrible ways by laying down his life for those who called themselves his friends. David hurled a rock towards his misshapen head and instead of ducking, he decided to let it strike him for the only cause that made any sense.

9

LAMECH'S APPEAL

"My name is Lamech, son of Methuselah. Please do not confuse me with the other Lamech who came your way a few generations ago."

The angel frowned, remembering the older namesake who, under no circumstances, would be allowed into Heaven. "So, what makes you think you deserve a celestial future?" the angel asked.

Lamech thought about his long life – not as long as his dad's, but long enough to have eventually fathered a studious son, Atrahasis. Standing at the gates of heaven, Lamech was able to view the world's future without the constraints of earthly life. He saw how Atrahasis became a trusted advisor to King Ziusudra. He felt pride as he watched his son captain a unique expedition of three ships to explore the Mediterranean Sea. Whilst collecting rare plants and animals, their home city was engulfed in a great flood. On his return, Atrahasis had gathered his collections together and set off for the city of Ur where he and his entourage were challenged whether they recognised the current Moon God (No-on) as sovereign in the city. If so, he had to accept being renamed by the guards. So Atrahasis, took the name Noah – the first of many forced Jewish name redesignations that Lamech could view stretching out into the centuries beyond.

Then Lamech thought about the life he had led. He could hardly claim celestial blessing because of the achievements of his son – just as he could not be blamed for the indiscretions of his ancestors. Before it was flooded, he lived in the city of Shuruppak where he had thrived following the Sumerian way of life. Like his neighbours, he would share in the annual work of harvesting the plentiful grain which was stored in the ziggurat that he had helped construct as a young man. He was despondent as he viewed the destruction of all they had built when the Mediterranean burst through the fragile, natural, shell-based mud wall to create what became the Black Sea. Surely, he argued, just because all his work in Shuruppak was destroyed could not be held against him by the judgemental angel?

The angel asked why he had waited so long before producing his famous son. Lamech reviewed his earlier life which had been spent, like most young Sumerian men, exploring their sexuality without attempting to create new life. He was puzzled by the angel's apparent displeasure at the variety of sexual practices that Sumerian civilization regarded as healthy. But he was heartened by the angelic smiles when he talked about his modelling clay sculptures that he would sell and his abilities in performing on the string instrument he had inherited from his parents. Apparently, heaven approves of art but is less keen on promiscuous sex. He was unable to figure out why, but accepted this if it meant he would be allowed through the gates.

"Did you do anything unique? Is there any activity that you undertook about which you are particularly proud?"

Lamech worried about this question. He did not think he had been an especially accomplished musician. His little clay pots were no different from thousands of others and his laboring in the fields was no different from that of all his friends and neighbors. He wondered what, if anything, he had taught his celebrated son. As a little boy, Atrahasis (or Noah as I suppose he should think of him now) had been fascinated by the fermentation process that allowed Lamech to produce the beer for which his neighbors often thanked him. Perhaps this is what had sparked Noah's scientific interests in the first place.

"I think I was one of the best brewers in the city," Lamech opined. The angel smiled and Lamech entered heaven.

10

THE CRYPTOGRAM

As a cryptologist, I rarely venture outside the bounds of the counter-intelligence service. Within this tiny World, I built up a worthy reputation as the man who broke the Honey Code (so called because the more you played around with it, the stickier the mess you found yourself in). So, when the unusual request was made from the Pakistani government to second a cryptologist to the Paleontology Department of the University of Karachi, I was offered the job.

When I arrived at the University, I was given the best rooms and made welcome. I am not used to such treatment. I was probably a little flattered but also a touch suspicious as to why no-one was prepared to discuss the object of my mission. Was I being softened up? If so, why?

The answer came the next day. I received an anonymous letter, written in the most childish code imaginable, asking me to indicate if I was prepared to undertake a little job on the side for which I would be paid most handsomely. The sign of acceptance was for me to open all my windows. Now I cannot deny that the offer of a large cash sum was not tempting. Cryptologists – even senior professionals like me – are not highly paid. What is more, I am no saint who could never do wrong. However, I had been immersed in a service guided by the Official Secrets Act. And although the Paleontology Department of the University of Karachi was scarcely a counter-espionage organization, my windows remained firmly shut.

The next day, I was introduced to Doctor Nazir. It soon became clear that the previous day's offer had been a test designed by Nazir to see whether I could be trusted. This annoyed me and I must admit that I never took to Nazir. By now, however, I was too curious about the nature of the work that I was to undertake to show my aggravation. The youthful academic was now keen to show that he had overwhelming confidence in me.

"You must understand," he stressed, "that competition between researchers is fierce and there are no lengths to which our enemies will not go to steal, undermine or destroy our work."

"Surely, academic research is all about the disinterested quest for truth?" I asked with an irony lost on Nazir.

"Believe me," came the reply, "there are no tricks that your counter-intelligence service could teach the academic World!"

I decided that Nazir had both a concern that his work would be plagiarized and an over-active imagination. Accepting the job meant that I had to put up with his melodrama. So, I was not surprised when Nazir rushed me to the airport that evening. Our arrival a few hours later in Jeddah was unobtrusive; although I did remark on the number of Urdu-speaking porters who offered their services as we walked out of the customs hall. Nazir waved them away and we took a taxi to a nearby hotel. I was glad of the air-conditioning. The heat outside was oppressive – even after sunset. "Tomorrow you shall see the code you need to break," Nazir announced. I could not sleep but dozed fitfully throughout the night.

At breakfast, Nazir introduced Doctor Kahn. I liked Kahn; he seemed less stuffy than Nazir. Kahn was a field archaeologist so, unlike Nazir and me, he had not spent most of his working life indoors. Nazir told me that the three of us were now partners in a great enterprise. I was quietly pleased to note how Kahn frowned at this statement.

"Doctor Kahn came across a remarkable discovery during his latest excavations," Nazir went on. "To interpret its significance, I was called in and I decided that what we had on our hands was the most important artefact ever found."

Nazir glanced around him: the room was half full of hotel guests finishing their meal. No-one was within earshot although I guessed that Nazir was worrying about bugging devices. However, he decided that the dining room was the safest place to divulge the great secret, so he continued. "We have found the remains of a script – fossilized!"

I thought about this for a moment. "You mean you have found a scroll, or something like that, which through a freak of atmosphere and soil conditions has become fossilized over the past few thousand years?"

Nazir shook his head vigorously. "No, no. Carbon dating

shows the fragment to date back approximately sixty million years."

Now it was my turn to start looking round the room. "You are saying that you have discovered written material pre-dating the appearance of humans on Earth."

Nazir nodded, "You've got it!"

I looked at Kahn. He was not reacting to this extraordinary claim. He just sat there smiling. I turned to him and said, "But you cannot figure out the meaning of the script, so that is my job." Kahn stood up. "Are you ready?" he asked.

I was expecting another trip maybe to some God-forsaken camp under an unbearable sun where I would work through the night under arc lights, attempting to figure out indecipherable inscriptions in the sand. Instead, we went to Kahn's room where I was presented with two extremely neat sheets of A4 paper on which a calligrapher's black ink had etched a beautiful, rhythmic pattern of shapes.

"This is what it says," Kahn told me. "We have transcribed it exactly on one sheet: the other contains alternatives, depending on how you interpret what appeared to us as random cracks and scratches in the original."

I set to work. The two men sat in silence. I told them that they could talk as it would not disturb me, but they had nothing to say. They just watched as I went through the normal procedures for simple decoding. It did not take long. The script was clearly not designed to remain secret – nothing like the Honey Code I assure you. After a few adjustments to my original model, the whole text fell easily into place, and I wrote it out in full in English. As I was doing it, I planned my own tiny, melodramatic gesture. Eventually, I turned to the two men.

"Gentlemen, I think I know where you found your fossil. If my assumption is correct, then my translation can only mean one thing. God did not instruct Moses in writing the Ten Commandments: Moses just found them. It took him forty days to decode: it has taken me two hours."

Since then, of course, everyone knows what has happened. The Saudi and Pakistani governments are locked in dispute as to where the broken tablets should be displayed. Kahn and Nazir have been launching vituperative attacks on each other: each claiming the other has stolen their intellectual property. The "Visitors from other stars" industry received a huge boost: the latest manifestation being a lurid film showing how several strikingly beautiful spacemen and women, bringing law and clean-living to our planet, were eaten by dinosaurs upon landing. The survivors hid, fell into lust and debauchery, and begat the human race. Personally, I have taken refuge in the more peaceful atmosphere of the old War Department.

11

CIRCUS

"In Africa, elephants are trapped by covered pits. When an elephant strays from the herd and falls into one, the rest of the herd immediately collects branches and rolls rocks down to construct ramps, trying hard to get it out. Originally kings used to tame them by rounding them up with horsemen, deceiving them about the length of the handmade trench with banks and ditches, and when they were enclosed, they were starved into submission."

Pliny the Elder

Throughout history, we know how folk heroes have been created out of quite unheroic characters. Robin Hood was almost certainly a feared highwayman, and his gang would rob passing travelers in England's midlands. Billy the Kid (Henry McCarty) was a cattle rustler who murdered at least nine men. George (later, Saint George) was a Greek soldier in the Roman army whose foreign background marked him as a potential traitor to be expelled from the army and executed. But the truth about the great folk heroes is usually kept well concealed to retain the essential mystique that can inspire future generations to acts of heroism or piety.

Nomadic folk pass on the tales of the forefathers by word of mouth. It was not until Ezra started writing about the nomadic families of Abraham of Ur that any recognizable Jewish history became apparent to the reading public. But circus folk retain the verbal traditions without recourse to the pen. When Pliny the Elder started writing about us and the animals we featured in our shows, many believe this marked the very beginnings of the circus. But we who maintain the word of mouth know stories that go back far earlier.

I do not know if I shall be sanctioned by daring to tell you what, previously, has been a jealously guarded secret told by fathers to their sons. But perhaps there comes a time when the truth should be given the light of day and not kept hidden within our travelling tents or spoken in hushed tones around the campfire.

When the Persians invaded Babylon in 539 BCE, their army was preceded by various artists and storytellers. This was a deliberate strategy to prepare the population for Cyrus, the incoming ruler, and the Achaemenid dynasty. One of these cultural forerunners was the circus. Their advertising campaign featured graffiti artists proclaiming how Babylon was found wanting when it came to the performing arts and offering the excitement of the circus to make up for what they had been missing. The fire eaters, Shadrach, Meshach, and

Abednego were star attractions who would give the audience a foretaste of what was on offer in the big tent by showing off in the streets beforehand. Kept strictly within the tent was the performance of the lion tamer, Daniel. His beasts imported from Egyptian traders in African animals, were especially valuable and would never be offered the temptation to escape by appearing outside the big tent.

We circus folk who live in tents are especially aware of the architecture of those who construct buildings. We notice how tyrants express themselves by erecting imposing walls, bare and plain, with little or no decoration. It has been the same throughout history whilst we maintain a long tradition of fine and refined art within our lovingly maintained caravans. Nebuchadnezzar, the Babylonian king, built palaces and fortifications designed to strike fear into the populace as the walls loomed high and grey over the city. They were erected in straight lines with sharp corners and with no notion of circular or rounded features. He was wary of these initial Persian interlopers – especially when he could see how popular they were amongst his people. He was particularly afraid of the graffiti artists who painted gaudy messages across his walls. Some proclaimed that his rule was "found wanting" as he failed to entertain or inspire those who lived in his realm. He gave orders to have the circus performers arrested on trumped up charges just to get them off the streets. Embellished stories of how they were mistreated were based upon the king's orders. In fact, they escaped punishment because Cyrus's army arrived, and Nebuchadnezzar took flight even before any military engagement could happen.

Cyrus and his army marched into Babylon unopposed. The people greeted him as the bringer of exciting artists, celebrated scholars, enlightened government as well as new buildings beautifully decorated with paintings – an architecture based upon curves! He gained particular popularity with the Judahites who had been exiled from their homeland forty-seven years before when the Babylonians had invaded northern Judea. Cyrus called their leaders to his court and asked if they would like to return to the city they regarded as their religious capital, Jerusalem. It was a meeting embellished by the performances of musicians, jugglers, acrobats, fire-eaters, and animal tamers. It was there that our forebears witnessed Cyrus issuing the famous Edict that authorized and encouraged the return of the exiled Judahites to the land of Judah and the rebuilding of the Temple in Jerusalem.

We circus people have always been on the lookout for new territory where we could perform. So, Daniel and his fire-eating colleagues joined the Jews returning to their ancient home. The problem of integrating Persian nomads into Jewish society was tricky. Jewish tribes seem to have a penchant for studying devotional texts in the quiet whereas we circus people enjoy live performance and noisy storytelling over a campfire. Eventually the Jews accepted us through the astute intercession of the Kohanim, the priestly family leading the rebuilding of the second Temple of Jerusalem. They revised the story of Daniel, the lion tamer, and the brothers Shadrach, Meshach, and Abednego and presented them as survivors from an imaginary fiery furnace built by the happily defeated king, Nebuchadnezzar. They were to be regarded as people especially protected by their God: so, the Book of Daniel became part of the folklore of Jews, Christians, and Muslims. But we circus people remember them as performers, just like us.

12

THE SUBMISSION

Daniel Jacobs, former sporting idol, was speaking to the Board of Enquiry. "... and I found the trip educational. My guide talked a lot about progress but pointed out that when the World held only four million people, three and a half million lived in permanent poverty. Nowadays, with seven billion people on Earth, the proportion has not changed at all." He cleared his throat and looked a little embarrassed, as if he had said something rude. Then he ploughed on. "What I am trying to say is that we don't change much: we still have the same needs be they physical or recreational. That was one of the lessons I learnt on the trip. Later, whilst the guide was having a break, I met Gabriel."

"I do not believe there are any female angels. They are all heavyweight wrestlers, and Gabriel is their champion. If you try and get to Heaven without an invitation, you are met with one of these bouncers. I had gone down to the river Styx to see whether it was true that there were no reflections when I felt a tap on my shoulder. I turned and there was Gabriel asking what I thought I was doing. I told him to mind his own business, and he smacked me in the mouth. The fight started, and the other angels soon gathered to watch the spectacle. Now I don't know whether he knew that I used to be the World Champion, but after a few throws I think he knew that it was not going to be such an easy contest. The problem was that every time I knocked him down, he got up stronger. It was only when he jumped on my back that I discovered his weakness. When he was not touching the ground, he seemed to lose his ability to apply powerful holds. But before I could put this knowledge to use, he got me in a terrible leg grip that I later discovered had dislocated my hip. It hurt worse than anything I had experienced. But I escaped, lifted him up and put him in my favorite submission hold. After a struggle, he cried out that I had won, so I dropped him in the Styx. The other angels fished him out and congratulated me on the bout."

"Gabriel was a bad loser. He was mad about getting wet and spat out that with my bust hip I would never wrestle again, and he was right. But the others calmed him down, pointing out that it was a fair fight and that I would obviously become one of the guards at the Main Gate after I had died. Gabriel looked puzzled and said, "Aren't you dead yet?" I told him that I was only on a trip, and that I hoped to go home soon. So that was when he made the deal with me. If I could set up the venue, he would send me his very best wrestlers to take on the finest that I could train. He is seeking revenge for his defeat, and I am trying to set up an alternative source of income now that I cannot fight professionally anymore."

"In my written submission, this is why I have been able to guarantee wrestling of the very highest standard. The contestants will attract thousands of tourists, television contracts and lots of trade for local business. I trust that this public enquiry will take these considerations into account and recommend the granting of planning permission for the building of my sports complex."

13

THE PLEA

Sergeant Potts looked dolefully at the people before his desk. "Are you all from the holiday camp?" he asked. They nodded and the man went on to tell Potts his version of events. The policeman had heard so many stories of quarrels, fights, and disputes from holidaymakers that he wondered sometimes whether they would all have been happier staying at home. The man finished his account and Potts stared at the swarthy youngster who was standing, disheveled, closest to the desk. "All right, young man, let's hear what you have to say."

"My name is Samson: everyone calls me Sammy. I am here with my parents. They will be in our tent worrying about where I am. Please let me get back to them," he pleaded.

"Not till you've told me what happened," Potts insisted. Sammy took a few deep breaths, composed himself, and then

| 50 |

spoke with a controlled nervousness that Potts had seen many times before.

"I met Della at the disco last week." Sammy pointed to the pretty girl beside him. "We got on really well, she is a great dancer. And she said that I made her laugh a lot. I do not think her family..." Sammy pointed to the rest of the group..."have much fun together. So, we started meeting during the day, walking down on the beach, and drinking lemonade at the camp café. I do not think that her family knew, nor cared, where Della was. My parents insist on knowing where I am whenever I go out. They know that I was going out for a walk with Della this afternoon: but they would be worried sick if they knew that I was in a police station. Please let me get back to them..."

"Listen, young man, no-one is going anywhere until I've heard what's been going on. So, carry on." Sammy looked over his shoulder at the two skinheads.

"When Della's two brothers came across her and me today, they taunted me with racist comments. Not only that... they made remarks about my long hair."

"What sort of remarks?"

"Well, I could not repeat the language that they used, it was most foul. But they implied that having long hair showed that all of us Sikhs were homosexuals."

"OK. What happened then?"

"Well, Della tried to get them to leave us alone. But they were not listening to her. They obviously objected strongly to my being with their sister. They called her a "slag" and pushed her away. Then they started punching me. Della shouted to them to stop, but they took no notice. She ran off to get help whilst these two threw me down in front of their tent and began kicking me. As you can see, they are both a lot larger than I am and I could not get away. Then one of them produced a razor. I had not been very scared until then, I just thought that they were like the normal louts that I see at school every day. But when I saw this cut-throat razor, I thought they were going to slash me. So, I ducked into their tent. I was not thinking where I was going, just anywhere to get away. They plunged in after me and pinned me down. I was screaming for help. The fat one sat on me, and the other one brought the razor right up to my face. Then he laughed and started shaving off my hair.

It was horrible. It really seemed to give them a thrill to do it. I stopped struggling because I was afraid that if I moved, he would cut my head. After a bit, he stopped to look at what he had done. I kicked out as hard as I could and must have knocked down the tent pole. The roof started to sink down, things started crashing to the ground, and the two of them dived for the door. I crawled out as best I could. Della must have found her parents whilst all this was going on because they saved me from any more humiliation by separating me from her brothers. Della's father asked his sons what was going on, and they said they had caught me stealing from their tent. They are liars. But he marched us all over to the police station as he believed them."

Potts did not like this sort of case. He could see that the Sikh kid had had some of his hair shaved off. He decided to do everything by the book. "Do you want to bring any charges against Della's brothers?" he asked. Sammy shook his head and said, "I just want to let my parents know where I am."

"All right," Potts said. "There is no evidence that you stole anything. But you did break the tent pole by your own admission. I shall be investigating whether there is a case against you for criminal damage to property."

Pott's words were like cold water rudely waking Sammy. He had been blind to the obvious, blind to his duty, blind to his true task. He shook his head. His parents had warned him what would happen if he went out with this white girl. Assuaging their feelings of a betrayed tradition, of broken family obligations, of improper conduct; this was the challenge. Only overcoming this could make him into a man. Pleading for their forgiveness would take every ounce of his fast-ebbing strength.

14

AMBITION

"My ambition is to be Pope." Peter was the outstanding novice at the old seminary. If any of his generation were to become the supreme pontiff, it was most likely to be him. "What is your ambition, Thomas?"

Thomas possessed a calm, contemplative character that contrasted sharply with his closest friend's brilliance. After a few moments thought, he replied.

"I'd like to see miraculous evidence of Christ on Earth."

--

Thirty years later, Peter had become famous as an academic writer and theologian. His great book on the significance and role of miracles was a source of inspiration to many, including Thomas. Even the College of Cardinals and successive Popes regarded it as a major contribution to the Faith: although none ever thought to invite the author to lead the Church.

So, although his wonderful intellect was widely recognized, Peter never achieved his ambition.

During the writing of the book, Peter had invited Thomas to go on the pilgrimage to Lourdes. Hoping for a miracle, Thomas had agreed. Looking for primary source material, Peter had gone with barely suppressed expectations. Most of the journey was spent in a gently swaying railway carriage. "Do you think that this is a Heavenly chariot?" Thomas asked, smiling. "Perhaps we would experience the process of discovery, the point of pilgrimage, if we were walking," Peter replied. So, for the final thirty miles, they took to the road. Thomas loved the open air, the breeze-cooled sun, the chatter, and dust of the town. Peter found the going increasingly difficult. His stride kept slowing down; so, Thomas offered to carry one of his backpacks.

Peter did not like to admit his weaknesses and refused all help. Their progress became more painful as they neared Lourdes. Thomas was excited as they got closer and wanted to break into a run. But Peter held him back. By the time that they reached the town center, Peter was exhausted. What should have been a joyous arrival turned into a tired anti-climax. Peter collapsed into his room whilst Thomas wandered around the sights. He felt frustrated that his friend had prevented the realization of his ambition. Thomas was annoyed with Peter. Their relationship was strained. Such a spirit was not conducive to sensing any miraculous presence at Lourdes.

Although they kept in touch sporadically over the next few years, eventually they lost contact. Seemingly forgotten by his seminary friend, Thomas had been the priest in a tiny village for thirty years. As he walked along the mountain track between the church and his house, he could hear the boys calling to each other in the woods. Although the villagers came to the Sunday service, he was finding it increasingly difficult to persuade the boys to attend his religious instruction lessons. They preferred to snare small animals in the woods: and as the village became poorer, the families encouraged them to catch the odd rabbit for the pot.

He called the boys all by name; and they came running over, keen to tell the priest of their latest and largest trap. But he asked them roughly why they had not been with him at the lesson that afternoon. They stood, looking at the dusty ground in silence. He really loved the children and could not stand seeing them upset when he knew it was their own parents who had sent them out into the woods. So, he dismissed them with a friendly pat on the head, as if in absolution but in fact as an act of contrition for his own brusqueness.

Over the previous three months he had been feeling distracted after Peter had written to him out of the blue. The surprise was partly because he had assumed that he would have long ago disappeared from the memory of the celebrated theologian. But the contents of the letter were even more astonishing to him. Peter had explained that a young boy named Joseph had been orphaned after his family were killed in a car crash. After the accident, Joseph had begun to experience extraordinary dreams – some of which seemed to be accurately prophetic. Psychologists and religious leaders were equally puzzled by the extreme clarity of the child's sleeping visions. Peter had been consulted as an authority on miraculous events. Whilst in Peter's care, Joseph's last dream had foreseen the coming of a miracle in a place which he described with such precision that it was not difficult to trace. Although he had never been anywhere near the vicinity, Joseph had had an intensely sensed experience of walking in the village where Thomas lived.

Peter had asked his old friend if it would be possible for Joseph to be given a home. The letter read: "The boy has no living relatives now. His lifeline to the future appears to be his visionary experiences. I feel that it is important that we allow him to be near wherever his dreams are leading him. None of us can understand what is happening in his mind. Perhaps it is the thoughts of a distant Deity, perhaps it is the breath of one nearby. Maybe it is the voice of the Devil, or it may be nothing at all except the hallucinations of a disturbed child. He needs some security: he needs to be treated the same as other children: he needs to feel more normal. Can you manage to have him "adopted", so to speak, near you? Obviously, the Church will pay all the expenses of the household that welcomes him."

As Thomas neared his cottage, he could hear Maria singing happily. She was his daughter, the result of an indiscretion some thirteen years before. The authorities outside the isolated village chose to ignore his straying from the path of chastity, and the villagers did not care. He had brought Maria up on his own, and as his paternal instincts had focused on her, he had found it easier to talk to all the children. She had attended his lessons that afternoon with her girl friends and one boy, the adopted child Joseph. She was fond of Joseph as he was very small and did not run in the woods with the rest of the boys. Thomas, on the other hand, found Joseph the only child with whom he could not converse. A sulky, intense child, Joseph seemed to treat the old priest with a mixture of hostility and suspicion that Thomas found hard to understand. The parents with whom Thomas had placed Joseph were a jovial couple with eight of their own children already. The father was the village carpenter and as poor as everyone else. So, the couple had been glad of the financial assistance that came with Joseph. When he had enquired as to how they were finding the newcomer, they had told him that Joseph rarely spoke to anyone in the house. As Joseph seemed to have become so uncommunicative, Thomas was pleasantly surprised when Maria announced that Joseph was on his way over to speak with him.

A few minutes later, the boy arrived. He said that he had questions about the lesson. Thomas was uncomfortable for, although he wanted the children to receive religious instruction, his own scholarship was not like Peter's. He knew that he could not readily answer more profound questions. Joseph asked about something that had only been mentioned in passing – what are stigmata? Thomas explained that they were the marks on the crucified Christ's body which do occasionally reappear on the bodies of living people now. Maria became excited and urged Joseph to show her father his marks. The boy opened his hands and both children stared, with expressions of amazement, at the upturned palms. It was as if they could see something faraway yet within his hands.

Thomas could see nothing. He looked at the children again to see whether they had decided to play a cruel practical joke upon him. But their eyes were lit with the flame of distant illusion. It was he who could not see. He looked down again at the child's hands. There was no mark on his skin. Thomas mused that perhaps there was some tradition where all was revealed only to the innocents. But he could not remember any such teaching. Joseph suddenly turned to the priest. "You see nothing, you are like all the other boys!" And with that, he rushed from the house, slamming the door as he left.

The evening was dominated by Maria refusing to speak to her father. Both were upset. They retired to bed early and Thomas slept fitfully. In the morning, he was awakened by Maria shouting to him from outside to come quickly. He hurried out and followed her up the path and into the wood. There, caught by his feet in the large trap, was Joseph. He had been whisked into the air and had been hanging upside down all night. He may have struck his head on the trunk of the tree so hard that he had died instantly: but if he had survived that, he was not strong enough to have lasted the long hours since. The boys were there, unsure what to do. "Cut him down!" Thomas called, his voice cracking. The children tried to untie the rope, but it was too tight. One produced a knife and cut his way through the cord. Little Joseph fell from the tree into the bush below. Maria rushed forward and pulled him from the thicket as brambles became entangled in his clothes and hair. Then, and only then, did Thomas finally realize his ambition and see the crown of thorns.

15

LEGACY

Romana was fun. Her Director of Studies at college regarded her as a nuisance. Her pranks kept getting her into trouble that the Director had to clear up afterwards. But she was a popular girl with lots of friends and, truth be told, her pranks never hurt anybody.

When Romana received a note requiring her attendance at the Director's study, she assumed it was to receive yet another reprimand. She was puzzled because she could not recall doing anything naughty in the previous week. Quite the contrary, she had spent most of the time in the history library studying the American Civil War. She had been writing about Abraham Lincoln in a way that had inadvertently infuriated her history tutor. The tutor had asked her to consider whether the great President was as wonderful a man as the Yankee historians described, or whether he was a genocidal maniac bent on the destruction of the south's culture as painted by contemporary Confederate accounts. Romana had compared his handwriting with the writing of others in 1860s United States and concluded, in line with the Journal of Abnormal Psychology, that the man showed no psychotic tendencies in this most personal evocation of character. She concluded that he was "normal" by mid-19th century standards: but the tutor was angry that she had introduced "damned psychology" into "serious history". She could not believe that her Director of Studies was going to tell her off for affronting the small-mindedness of the history tutor.

"Sit down, I have something to tell you." This did not sound good. She went through all the things she might be told that could upset her. Both her parents had died in the crash two years ago; so, she did not believe that anything worse could be in store. She started making a mental note of all the pranks that she had performed since then. She understood very well they had been a childish reaction to the loss of her mum and dad, and she also knew that her Director of Studies pitched the required reprimands in the light of her loss.

"Do you know Julius Remus?" Romana frowned. Was he a student? Was he the man who had nearly knocked her off her bike the day before when he opened his car door and blamed her, in a stream of racist and sexist insults, for damaging his shiny Alfa-Romeo? She wracked her brains, but the name meant nothing to her. She shook her head.

"I have to tell you that his legal firm have been in touch after tracking you down." Now this sounded even worse. Was there some law she had broken? It must be bad for a law firm to be chasing her. She took a deep breath, preparing for whatever the next awful moment in her life was about to be presented.

"Their client, Julius Remus, has died." Now how could that be her fault? She did not even know who he was. She was getting ready to protest her innocence.

"His estate has been left to his nearest living relative. The lawyers have discovered, after considerable research, that you are in line to receive his inheritance. Romana looked intently at the Director. If anyone else had said this, she would have known it was a practical joke. In bad taste, but nonetheless, quite funny to think of her as a wealthy woman. But the Director was not smiling. She seemed very serious as if she had imparted important news that needed to be better understood.

"I have a sealed letter here that is addressed to you. The university authorities have been given some advance notice of its contents. I have been authorized to offer you any assistance that you may like from our legal department once you have read your letter." Romana took the letter and, unceremoniously, tore it open. After reading the single paragraph, she shook her head in disbelief. A few moments passed in stunned silence. Then the Director stood up and held out her hand. Unsure how to respond, Romana also stood and grasped it.

"I understand that congratulations are in order. I hope you realize the responsibilities that always accompany great wealth." Romana nodded; quietly thanked the woman and walked out in a daze.

--

For the next two days she did not call the phone number of the legal firm. Romana could not bring herself to speak to the lawyers. She was almost too afraid to hear what awaited her. Years later she wondered why the prospect of huge riches had not made her happy and excited. It was as if she already sensed that the radical changes awaiting her would disrupt the equilibrium that she had struggled to achieve after her parents' untimely death. She confided in her gentle, Icelandic boyfriend, Njáll. He gave her a cuddle and told her that he would always stand by her – even if she was a millionaire. She smiled but knew that being extremely rich could easily destroy the easygoing relationships enjoyed by equally indebted university students.

They spent a quiet day writing down the pros and cons of being wealthy. Romana wrote the cons in her florid hand – there were not many. Njáll wrote with his beautiful calligraphy a whole page of pros. After a rambling but inconclusive joint reflection upon what handwriting could tell them about their personalities, Romana summoned up the courage to make the phone call. The head of the legal firm advised that she travel down to the city office where all the details could be explained, and various documents signed and witnessed. She asked Njáll to accompany her. As a third-year law student, he might help if she got lost trying to follow what was happening.

Njáll did not need to explain anything. The last will and testament of Julius Remus was clear and simple. His nearest surviving relative was to inherit his entire estate whose contents were listed on an attached sheet of paper. The man had a house in New Orleans whose contents had an estimated worth of several million dollars. The house itself had a similar evaluation. His money was secreted in a series of savings accounts, also worth several million dollars. But most remarkable, and without a price tag, was the document that showed that he was the owner of Sclave, an entire, volcanic, Pacific Island. The head of the firm explained that the deceased had come from a French slave-owning family in Virginia. During the Civil War, Julius's distant ancestor had seen which way the war was going. He had the foresight to cash in much of his family's fortune and start buying the Pacific outpost where he believed, with some intuitive feel for trade, that a fortune could be made from exporting exotic fruit. Over the coming decades, the family had acquired every square meter of the island – so now Sclave was one hundred percent owned, freehold, by the astonished Romana.

"We would be glad to act as your legal representatives with regard to any transactions or contractual obligations into which you may wish to enter in future." Romana looked at Njáll to see if he was going to react to this offer. He stared meaningfully at her whilst shaking his head very slightly. So, she thanked the lawyer for his kind offer and said she would think about it. He looked disappointed but handed her the will and asked her just to sign the document that acknowledged receipt. She gave it to Njáll to read and he seemed satisfied that it was just as described. She signed, shook the lawyer's hand and, grasping the will in one hand and holding Njáll's with the other, left the office.

Following Njáll's advice to employ her own lawyer to ensure that her interests were protected, Romana went to the old gentleman, a family friend, who had handled the affairs after her parents' death. He told her that the sheer size of her newly acquired estate meant that he would not be able to handle it all on his own. Such an admission simply gave her further reason to trust him. And, sure enough, over the following month, all the Remus accounts were transferred into accounts in her name and the title to Sclave was recorded as hers and hers alone.

"What do we know about Sclave?" Njáll asked one afternoon. They had continued their university studies as best they could but had not had the time to discover anything about the island. Romana tried looking it up on the Internet but found nothing except the word itself seemed to be a shortened form of the French 'esclaves', meaning slaves.

"You have the money to travel over there to see the place with your own eyes," Njáll pointed out. Truth be told, it had not registered in her mind that this was the case. She still felt as if she was a student who carefully watched how much she was buying whenever she visited the supermarket; automatically choosing cheaper lines to save money. Njáll wondered whether she should engage a travel agent to purchase all the tickets required so that she did not need to worry about working it all out. After taking his advice, she experienced an enormous sense of relief as if a great weight had been lifted from her chest. The very first benefits of wealth had appeared.

Although she wanted Njáll to come with her, he said he first needed to go to see his ageing parents. She felt another pang of loss; at least he had parents to visit. They parted at the airport and Njáll watched her flight take off, wondering if she was leaving him for good as she was drawn, inevitably, into the realm of the super-rich. Nothing could have been further from the truth.

--

Romana decided to stay a few days in Papeete. To access Sclave, she would have to engage a local fisherman or pearl diver to take her from Tahiti as Sclave had no airstrip. Her French was not good enough to explain why she wanted to visit this distant little island, but as she had no hesitation in paying the exorbitant sum requested, she had no difficulty in obtaining the services of Jean-Baptiste Baroque. She smiled at his surname because his handwriting was so decorative. On the phone to Njáll that night, she said that she thought clinical psychologists would have had a field day trying to disentangle any meaning from the loops and swirls of Jean-Baptiste Baroque's writing.

The boat journey was idyllic. The ocean was quiet, and Jean-Baptiste talked slowly in English or in some form of pidgin English that Romana found easy to follow. She explained to him how Julius Remus's death had thrown her into this Pacific trip. He told her all he knew about Sclave.

"The islanders keep themselves to themselves. There are very few of them. Every year some will leave Sclave and others will return. Sometimes the boys return with a bride and that way there have been children on the island over the past centuries. But they retain a very simple culture with fruit and vegetable growing at its heart. They do not use machinery and plough with cattle or by hand. You will like them; they are very friendly. But simple ... you understand? They all knew Julius Remus as he visited every year. But they do not know about you yet. You will need to talk with the elders so that they understand that Julius has died."

She asked who the elders were. He smiled and explained: "The couple I thought I'd leave you with are researchers from Auckland. They are writing a book about the cargo cults of the Pacific and will be able to describe the function of the elders better than me. But I can tell you that the cargo cult community live in the woods beside the extinct volcano, and they elect their own elders. On the coast is where the people who have worked or travelled abroad live. You will easily see the difference. But if you want to talk with those in the woods, you'll need to meet the elders first or no one will want to speak with you."

Jean-Baptiste docked easily beside the fishing boats and was greeted by a small crowd who obviously knew him well. The children shouted his name "Jean-Baptiste! Jean-Baptiste!" and he reached into his pockets and pulled out a shower of sweets that he threw into the air with a laugh. She did not know why but she did not expect the research couple to be black- skinned like her and Jean-Baptiste. But they introduced themselves as Joseph and Mary and had all the appearance of a Melanesian, or maybe Mauri, husband and wife. They already knew about Julius Remus's death and her inheritance and seemed anxious in case she would not agree to them continuing their research on her island. She quickly reassured them and asked them to explain the cargo cult that had obviously existed on Sclave for many years.

"We will take you to meet the elders but need to warn you that they regarded Remus as a magician. They believe he magically increased their fruit crops by introducing chemical fertilizers. They saw these as proof of his supernatural powers. The only reason why they did not accord him the status of a god is because, according to their religion, God will appear like a Christlike, white figure that they learnt about from nineteenth century missionaries. Like you and us, Remus was not white."

In the next few days, after Jean-Baptiste had returned to Tahiti, Romana walked around her island. She noticed the tiny crucifixes made of wood affixed to the gravestones, the strange offerings of fruit and children's toys in paniers beside the road ready to greet any visiting deity, and the wooden chapel without glazed windows that looked out onto the Pacific that remained empty with no sign that the building had ever welcomed any congregants. Joseph and Mary introduced her to the elders – just twelve very old men who sat on rickety, wooden chairs in the dust of the village lying beneath the extinct volcano. Mary explained to them that Julius Remus had died, and that Romana was now the new owner. They talked between themselves and then asked Joseph whether Romana was as great a magician as Julius.

"The problem," Mary explained later, "is that the chemical fertilizers have destroyed the soil. So, they now believe the drop in their crop yield is due to the decline in Julius Remus's health and his death. They are looking to you to bring about a magical transformation."

--

A week later, when Jean-Baptiste Baroque was due to return to collect Romana, she had taken it into her head to take a trek up the mountain. Joseph and Mary accompanied her as they said the route was rocky and no one should attempt it alone. The view from the summit was spectacular and the ocean spread out like a perfect, blue carpet to the horizon in every direction. As they descended, they could see Jean-Baptiste's boat moored in the bay. He was waiting for them at Joseph and Mary's house.

"There's a surprise visitor for you," he announced to Romana. "He went off to meet you, but I think he may have gone through the woods instead of using the coastal trail."

Romana, Joseph and Mary set off to see who the surprise visitor could be. The elders met them with gratitude in their eyes, thanking Romana for sending the white god to resurrect their declining food supply. And there, before the makeshift church, they had erected a full-size crucifix upon which they had nailed Njáll.

16

THE SECRET OF THE PILLOW

The fascination I have for him is not based upon appearance. True, he made an instant impression: tall and handsome with muscles that seemed to ripple in the sunshine as he walked up the beach. He smiled at me, and I felt strongly attracted: and the feeling seemed to be mutual. I know that other women look at him as he paces along with that relaxed gait of his. I have seen men gaze at him with admiration. His whole body gives off a warm glow that makes me feel good inside. But, despite all these merits, they are not what fascinate me about him.

He is a sensuous and generous lover. His attentions are the most welcome that I have ever received. After making love, he likes to wander into the kitchen and prepare a meal. His talents there are considerable. I cannot recall tasting anything he has cooked which has not been a delight. When we have invited guests to our home, it is always he who creates the meal with a skill that I suspect that few chefs can match. But despite all these merits, they are not what fascinate me about him.

The first time I heard him play the violin, I was awestruck by the sheer brilliance of his musicianship. "When did you learn to play like that?" I asked. He just shrugged his shoulders and asserted that almost anyone could play like that if they wanted to. It was just that they convinced themselves that they could not at an early age and suffered from self-imposed barriers for the rest of their lives. Sometimes he sings quietly to himself, he has a most beautiful voice. But despite all these merits, they are not what fascinate me about him.

I do not fully understand the work that he does. I know his business empire includes media outlets and that he pays them a great deal of attention. Our house has seen a succession of famous politicians and corporate bosses seeking his advice and support. He radiates an extraordinary authority over them as they listen attentively to his words and counsel. I am well aware that some women find powerful men incredibly attractive. And there have been many who have cast their charms his way. I cannot imagine anyone with greater charisma. But despite all these merits, they are not what fascinate me about him.

Every morning, he stretches himself and climbs lazily out of bed before taking a shower. I lie there waiting for him to leave the bedroom. Then I sit up and inspect his pillow. And there, without fail, I can see the imprint of his head with their two invisible but fascinating horns.

17

THE WIDE ATTENTION
SPAN

Driving cosmic systems is tiring.

There is so much to consider. Bashing a couple of quasars together can be quite fun, provided there is no possibility of life forms in the immediate vicinity. Zipping in and out of black holes can be exhilarating although, once you've done it a few trillion times, it can get boring.

I admit that my attention was drawn away from your planet last century ... yours is not the only civilization which I attend. In fact, most recently, I can honestly say that I could have done with a bit of help because – despite your funny trinitarians – there's only one of me.

Some of you think I've chosen you as being special and so believe I've been asleep at the wheel by allowing some of the more monstrous specimens of humankind to inflict massive pain and suffering upon millions of innocent people. And, if

I'm brutally honest with myself (and how can I be anything but?) I may have dozed a bit after quite a big piece of work in a galaxy far away from Earth. In my defense I would point out that the work saved a far more advanced civilization than has yet to evolve on your planet. There, the entities all live happily for centuries underwater – and it was the water that was evaporating because of the expanding red giant nearby that threatened them. But whilst I was helping save them, I find you let your genocidal tendencies get the better of you. I turn my back just for a few years and what do I find?!

I wish I could provide you with lessons from the underwater civilization. Their leaders have absolutely no notion of being superior to their peers. Their technology is so much further advanced than yours and their understanding of the world around them so much more profound that, on second thoughts, I doubt if you would yet know how to learn from them. There are occasions when I reluctantly admit that I am tempted to just let you get on with your ridiculous path to self-destruction. I look at your current crop of leaders and cannot but help thinking "Oh! Go on! Get on with it. It's your future you seem to be intent upon obliterating."

But then I look again and find many fine examples of humanity worthy of saving. Little children chasing butterflies, fishermen afraid they won't make it back to port as the storm approaches, the solo violinist performing to a rapt audience, friends' laughter at a funny joke. That red giant is getting bigger again: I'll have to decide which planet's inhabitants most deserve my attention.

18

CHOSEN PEOPLE

Parisian Gerald knew that he had to make the decision. He felt that he loved both twins, but they had insisted that he choose between them. He could only marry one, but both had told him that they would rather die than be rejected. The next day, he chose one. That night, the other committed suicide.

Imagine how he feels now.

But that is nothing ....

Fatma was starving to death. Her two surviving children clung to her under the bitter Sudan sun. In her hand she held sixteen grains of rice perhaps enough for one child to survive for one more day. Eight grains each, and she knew that neither would be with her that evening. She slowly fed the grains into one mouth. She chose one, the other died in the afternoon.

Imagine how she feels.

But that is nothing ....

Rebecca was desperate and exhausted after two weeks in the cattle truck. Beaten from the train with a few hundred other survivors, the guard demanded that she choose which of her two children she would take into the camp, and which would take their place in the other queue. She chose and, wide-eyed, her little son was dragged away from the outstretched fingers of his dying mother. He was gassed that morning.

Imagine how she feels.

But that is nothing ....

I created the Universe and all its creatures. Humans evolved and demanded that I choose between them. Rather than watch them destroy each other, I chose one People to establish my Commandments. And now you have an inkling of how I felt as I made the choice.

19

THE SERAPH SPEAKS

There are eight of us. As far as I remember, there have always been eight of us. We are given names by others but, between us, we do not bother with names. I am number five and suspect that numbers six, seven and eight regard number one, two, three and four with as much suspicion as I have. But we do not speak of such things. In fact, none of us speak at all.

I have always found it puzzling that religious folk hold we seraphim in such high regard. To make them happy, there are always four of us on duty flying about the throne singing "holy, holy, holy." The four who are off duty are free to meditate and study and reflect upon all that we see, hear, and know. When it is my turn to fly around the throne, I reckon I can outdo the other three with the volume of my "holy, holy, holy". But when we are off duty, I am unsure if my colleagues share the same discomfort with our lot that has been increasing in my mind over the past centuries.

To retain the tradition of remaining dumb and keeping our vocal cords purely for singing "holy, holy, holy", I have never discussed the situation with any of the other seven. I am not even sure that they are aware of the cause of my disturbed state. When they fly, none of them appear to have any concerns as they streak around emitting transcendental light beneath the divine throne. Listening to the commentaries of the world's learned men (although almost no women do this), many of the theologically inclined seem to believe that the light of the world is merely the reflection of the light that we generate. Whatever wisdom we have acquired over the past millennia, it is obvious to seraphim (and everyone other than the theologically inclined) that it is only the sun that provides all the light and heat for the Earth.

It has also become increasingly obvious, therefore, that all the light that we eight generate has little or no bearing upon the energy requirements of the planet's inhabitants. The spectacle that we create with our burning light displays is so intense that humans are unable to see us, or anything beyond us. I suspect that this is why they regard our light emissions as having divine significance – they see us as brighter than the sun!

The truth may be harder to bear. They all crave to be able to cast their eyes upon the divine presence and may even be envious of our unique position in being able to fly around the throne and see what they wish that they could see. Perhaps it is best that the eight of us remain silent – even with each other – as we alone know that the throne is empty.

20 |

BOOK TWO: NEW TALES

1. The translator
2. The rings of Diomede
3. Lost in translation
4. Freelance
5. Angela
6. Keeping mum
7. The cube
8. Quiz
9. Angelic host
10. High rise
11. A tail to tell
12. Etiquette
13. Grendon
14. Heads
15. Juarez

21

THE TRANSLATOR

There was always going to be trouble once the Women's Council decided to build a mountainside pumping station. The krop birds that ruled the high ground were bound to resist. But once the Council makes a decision it is rare for it to retreat. Many women died constructing the pathway to the foothills and the pumping station itself. You can still see their skeletal remains having had their flesh stripped by the krop flocks.

We all know that every tripedal ends up as krop fodder. But most of us can look forward to a long life before we are dispensed with. I knew some of the women who were killed by the krops: and they were young and fit. It was a terrible waste of youth: but like all the other men in our Pumping Station I did not dare criticize the Council. We just got on with our routines, pumping the women when they came in for an energy top-up, bearing the children and running the pumping station schools and hospitals.

My own work as a teacher has always been a joy. With our tripartite brains, we tripedals have the capacity for intellectual, emotional, and practical development that eludes simpler bipedals like the krops. I subscribe to the theory that all higher life forms are bound to evolve tripedally as I can conceive of no more efficient body structure than ours. With our three legs driving our three wheels, our three faces with an eye in each face giving us all-round vision, three ears giving us all-round hearing, three mouths giving us the capacity to undertake three conversations at once – who could believe that anything better could develop? Of course, we cannot match the krops for speed as they can fly but they only have two wings instead of our three arms, their two talons can only snatch whereas our three-fingered hands can manipulate tools, and their two-hemisphere brain only provides them with the capacity to feel and survive. Most disgusting of all is the way that they consume nutrients. They eat flesh through their mouths! Our nutrient baths allow us to imbibe nutrients through our skin: and the sensation of sitting in a bath of finely minced fish has always been one of our greatest pleasure.

I suppose it was bound to happen eventually. We had observed the primitive life forms on the planet Earth for several hundred years. When they discovered early m-drive we knew that they would find their way to our solar system in time. My own work as a teacher/translator involved learning their languages as a special study. So, when they arrived, the Council ordered me to be amongst the greeting party. I was anxious because I knew they tend to resort to using primitive weapons when scared: and we had strict orders not to have them kropped. So, their landing near the mountain had to be treated as a defense project because of proximity to the krop nests. We travelled to the site of the landing protected only by anti-krop powder cannons puffing away overhead. The cloud of powder was thrown over the Earth ship to protect them and I was designated to communicate with the travelers. I explained to them that the cloud was for all our protection and that when they emerged, we would defend them against krops. But they seemed reluctant to leave their ship.

Eventually they came out slowly. My companions – mainly women who had never studied extra-terrestrial forms – were amused by these strange bipeds. Although about the same height and weight as us, their funny feet had failed to develop wheels so they could hardly move across the land. I asked if they would mind if we lifted them up to carry them to the new pumping station, as exposure in the open was dangerous. They consented and I carried one of their females: she told me her name was Amanda.

The reception committee at the pumping station was an impressive sight. The President herself came to welcome the guests and I translated her words. I assumed that Amanda or her female companion was their leader and was surprised when a male stepped forward to respond to our greeting. He said his name was Fred and that his party of four had come in peace to make friends across the galaxy. His first question was aimed at me. He wanted to know how I could speak his language. But our President required me to translate her words first. She explained that as guests they were welcome to use the facilities at the mountain pumping station, but they should not walk around with loaded weapons in case of accidents. Fred seemed suspicious and reluctant but, after consulting with Amanda, decided that he should accept the President's conditions. Perhaps the small party of Presidential guards holding powder-loaded puffers behind them would have persuaded him anyway. But Amanda seemed to be his sensible guide, so enforcement proved unnecessary.

As the all-female Presidential party required energy boosting, the young bucks came out and gave them a good pumping. The Earth visitors looked on horrified. Amanda asked if this sexual activity always took place in public. I had to explain that on our world sexual activity, as she understood it, took place between males who impregnated each other and gave birth a year later. The activity she was witnessing was what she would call re-fueling. I offered to provide her with the experience, but she refused, and her cheeks took on a peculiar red hue. The Presidential party made off, leaving us with the practical problems of accommodating the quaint quartet of visitors. The four of them, Amanda, Fred, Sue, and Peter, obviously required nutrients and were tired. I offered them fish, which they politely refused. They said they carried their own food supply. We provided them with a private room so they could engage in their revolting habit of placing hard nutrients inside their tiny mouths, biting them with krop-like teeth, and swallowing the contents. None of us could stand being in the same room. Afterwards, Amanda told me that they needed to sleep. Unlike us, these humans required flat, soft surfaces to lie on. Then they shut both their eyes and fall unconscious! We provided them with what they needed and, although tired, I rested outside their room with one eye open in case they required further assistance.

I am sure that Sue and Peter left their room whilst I was taking a fish bath. On my return, I looked inside their room and could only see Amanda and Fred asleep. I woke them up to ask where their companions had gone but both claimed ignorance. I quickly scanned the station's viseo record and discovered that they had walked to the pumping station exit, taken their side arms from the locker, and exited. The red sun had already set, and the white sun was in the sky. I raised the alarm. I knew the two of them could not survive without protection. I explained to Amanda and Fred that their colleagues were in danger and that we would have to organise a rescue party if it was not already too late. Fred wanted to join the party, but I told him that he would slow us down. He was not happy but accepted the situation.

"Why do you think they made off like this?" I asked.

"We are meant to be exploring the galaxy," Fred answered. "Peter has always been impatient to get on with it and Sue is his partner."

We found the pair of them not far from the station. The krops had stripped them clean. There were signs that they had discharged their firearms – an action which would merely have infuriated a full-size krop. We brought back their remains and Amanda was extremely upset. Fred was speechless and I was in trouble. A Presidential order was delivered requiring that I account for my failure to guard and protect our guests. Fred and Amanda were asked to attend the court hearing as primary witnesses.

At the hearing, I had the unpleasant job of acting as defendant whilst providing translations and explanations to our guests. The other translators who could have attended were all otherwise engaged in work on the other side of the planet. The Presidential Representative, an elderly woman whom no one wished to pump, was the judge. She knew that she would soon become krop fodder, so her perception of Peter's and Sue's fate was certainly biased by awareness of her own near future. Whatever the reason, she expressed horror at my failing and said she could not understand how I could have neglected my sentinel duties for a fish bath. My defense, that I had no sentinel duties and had voluntarily placed myself near the guests in case they wished to speak to anyone, was rejected. I was ordered to leave the school for three trimesters and to provide pumping services for elderly women.

It was near the end of the third trimester that the same Presidential Representative wheeled herself into the pumping station. I was already exhausted by the exertions of the day and groaned inwardly when I saw her head towards me. The young bucks cleared a path for her, audibly commenting that she was on her last wheels and hoping that she would soon enjoy her final krop meeting. She ignored their jibes and demanded a full top-up from me. It was at this point that my pump drive just failed me. The bucks looked at one another and repeated their hopes for my future, my final krop meeting. The Presidential Representative was furious and demanded that I carry out my punishment or there would be terrible consequences.

But it was no use. I could not get aroused, and her threats made it even worse for me. She posted a formal complaint against me; then made off towards the next pumping station. She must have finally run out of energy along the road as her skeleton was discovered the next day by a fish convoy.

Trouble arrived when a three-women panel came to hear the posted complaint. I knew that the result was likely to be expulsion from the pumping station and exposure to the krop flock. I suppose that I was resigned to the inevitable as it was now clear that my arousal rate was so low that most women would regard me as nothing but spent fuel. I countered with the argument that I was more use to them as a teacher and translator; but I knew that women would regard this as of only secondary importance – especially as my failure had resulted in the death of one of their companions. To my surprise, I was saved by the krops!! Fred and Amanda had said they wished to return to their home planet. But whilst I was before the panel, the krops decided to attack their ship. Although protected by a light dusting, a full-blown flock attack shifted the cloud long enough for the ship to be exposed. Many krops collapsed beside the stricken ship, but it was so badly damaged that it could never take our guests back to Earth. The President then ordered one of our galactic ships to take them home. The pilot and navigator needed an interpreter to communicate with the two passengers; so, the President herself ordered the panel to sentence me to accompany Fred and Amanda and make myself available to the Earth authorities to explain what had happened to their companions.

She assumed that Earth's punishment system would dispose of me with the same efficiency as the krops.

Our arrival on Earth was greeted by hundreds of humans. Fred and Amanda emerged from the galactic ship and waved to the crowds. I followed a few minutes later and was struck by the silence that fell across those watching. They were evidently astonished by the appearance of so different a creature.

The pilot called out to me. "The President does not want any of our technology to be made available to these bipeds. So, we shall leave you now." And with those words, she took off leaving me stranded.

The crowd seemed to take a huge intake of breath as the ship disappeared from the planet; then they all gazed in my direction. Fred and Amanda led me through to a reception committee where I was well treated. I was asked what I required for sustenance; I was given a pleasant greeting message from their President and assured by Fred and Amanda that all my needs would be catered for. It was as if they did not recognize that my exile was a punishment.

The following month was a most peculiar experience. The Astronautics Science Team wanted to inspect my body but was required to ask my permission, as I was able to speak their language. I noticed that other creatures are examined and even vivisected without permission if they could not communicate. So perhaps it was fortunate that I had studied their broadcasts so attentively when younger. I allowed them to poke around but I drew the line at vivisection! Amanda visited me frequently and seemed concerned that I should be happy and not feel what she described as homesick. The

Earth's media teams who wanted to show me on their television channels also visited me. Amanda told me that within weeks I had become the most viewed image worldwide. She asked if I liked being famous. My response was recorded and listened to by several billion humans.

I had not been wasting my time during the first month. All my Earth studies had been undertaken whilst living at the other end of the galaxy. Here was an opportunity to study these strange human subjects at close range. I read many of their books, three at a time. I listened to broadcasts in several of their languages, three at a time. And I conversed with many of their thinkers and leaders (almost entirely mutually exclusive groups), usually three at a time. I was struck by the variety of processes developed for final disposal of bodies. There was no symbiotic relationship as we had with our krops where we provided them with food, and they provided us with a hygienic disposal system. I was intrigued by what humans called religion and its relationship to body disposal. Religious language was obviously a sophisticated code describing basic truths and aspirations. I was asked about what they called "fame", and it was interpreted as an encrypted religious message teaching humans how a more advanced civilization could organize themselves.

I said, "We are born, and we are kropped: what we do between is largely determined by our women who decide about who should be famous." Then I added: "In our culture, women see pumping as a matter of life and death whereas in yours it seems to be even more important."

The headlines read 'Alien says sex is more important than

life or death' and 'Make love or die is message from the stars.' Amanda came for a visit to warn me about how my words could be misinterpreted.

"People have their own agendas and will take anything you say to confirm their view, no matter how you phrase your sentences."

She described the growing sect calling itself the kroppers. "They believe that death can be defeated if they can kill death's representatives, the krops. They identify krops with the devil but have no idea what a krop is. Now some are saying that you are the krop's representative on Earth."

I did not like the sound of that. "You mean there is a cult whose aim is to murder me?" She nodded and, for the first time, I felt a craving for a ship of women to take me back to a familiar pumping station.

Fortunately, when I was kidnapped, it was not by the kroppers. The mastermind behind the operation had obviously planned meticulously. I was being well protected by the authorities, but we all know there is no such thing as perfect security. Every system has flaws, and the kidnappers knew exactly how to exploit the one surrounding me. I was bundled into a waiting vehicle and driven off into the night. I was placed inside a large, carefully prepared enclosure. It contained a house and garden and a huge bath continuously supplied with minced fish. I was watched by banks of cameras placed strategically everywhere within the enclosure. Despite the warnings about kroppers, I was not afraid because it was clear that if they had wanted me dead, they would not have made such an effort to meet all my needs.

The following month turned out to be quite exhilarating. Into the enclosure each day, a young woman would appear and request a full pumping. First out of curiosity I would provide her with what she wanted; but after a few days I found that I was quite enjoying the sensation. After my trimesters with elderly tripedals, sessions with these soft-skinned bipeds were an extremely pleasant improvement. Day after day, women would appear with the same request, and I was more than happy to respond. I began to feel a little as I had when, years before, I had served as a young buck in the Central Pumping Station. I had no idea that the cameras monitoring me were recording the sessions for pornographic sales.

After a month, I was traced by the authorities and "rescued" (although by then I was not really looking for rescue). The owner of the enclosure and media channel through which he was selling the videoed sessions was arrested; but quickly let off when he donated a substantial proportion of profits to the fund promoting the incumbent president in the upcoming election. More interestingly, Amanda informed me that several of the women whom I had serviced had become pregnant! So, at a molecular level, it seems that we have more in common than I thought.

The kropper attack was more frightening. Amanda told me that Fred had joined the sect. He had suffered from some sort of guilt complex following the death of Sue and Pete. This had been transferred to me during the trial and he saw the kroppers as the only people who understood his need to take his revenge on me. His knowledge of the authority's security system gave the lynch mob access, and they overpowered the guards outside my apartment. Fortunately, I retained a small supply of anti-krop powder secreted in my anal cavity: so, when they entered the room, a blast from my bottom disabled them instantly.

The trial of the kroppers was broadcast and their long prison sentence convinced many potential sect members that they were martyrs for a just cause and that my death was the only way to appease their strange gods. Amanda's visits became more frequent as she worried about my future. I found her concern quite appealing. I had to admit to a growing attraction towards this young woman – quite unlike what I felt towards the supply of females provided by my erstwhile captors. She seemed to appreciate me for what I was, a committed teacher/translator, not just a thrusting machine!

I should have guessed that my home planet's monitoring system would be following my progress. It seems that their Evaluation Panel concluded that I was no longer suffering the punishment I deserved and that I required a more severe taste of their displeasure. However, it was noted that I appeared to have regained my pumping capacity and was, therefore, of more use back home than on Earth. One group on the Panel argued that I should be returned for a further trimester of pumping for their elderly members. Others argued that I should be visited by a punishment party and left on Earth with my wheels disabled. What no one anticipated was the revolution which overthrew the all-women government. It was peaceful but highly effective. The team at the mountainside station started it; but coordinated action across all pumping stations brought down the government in less than the waning of two suns. The men refused to provide their services to any women unless I was returned, unscathed. They demanded that I should have no further punishment meted out for what the men saw as an entirely innocent action on my part in my failure to service the old Presidential Representative. Imagine my surprise when the galactic ship appeared with a mixed crew of men and women!

I was informed of the developments back home and told that my return as a celebrity would bring the revolution to a successful conclusion. My role as a teacher would be confirmed and I would be able to resume my duties just as soon as the parents agreed to have me back as their children's teacher. I discussed my situation with Amanda and shared my fear that I might never be able to become a teacher again. "Why not?" she asked. I explained: "Teachers are traditionally seen as leading peaceful, quiet, anonymous lives. Those in the public eye are seen as loud, vociferous, and mere propagandists or politicians. Teachers are seen as intelligent and thoughtful: those in the public eye are seen as mere entertainers, usually stupid, and quite unfit to be in education. If I am to be returned as a celebrity, no parents will want their children taught by me."

I talked with the 'rescue party'. Their leader, an old friend and fellow teacher who had headed the revolt in the Central Pumping Station, listened attentively. He appreciated my concern as he was now in the public eye so doubted if he could resume his teaching. I persuaded them to leave me on Earth as I was now expecting to be father to several children about to be born to a series of human women.

"Fathers should be available to their children," I asserted.

"How else will they learn of our traditions and mores?" The 'rescue party' agreed although I dared not admit the true reason for my wish to remain on Earth. Amanda was now the sole object of my attention and affection. I sensed that her feelings towards me were also amorous and becoming more intense. With Fred in prison, she was the sole surviving member of the original exploration party able to visit me. And the authorities ensured that she could come and go as she wished, so we were seeing one another almost every day.

The authorities were keen to engage the rescue party in a dialogue concerning advanced technology. They were even keener to inspect the ship and its inter-galactic drive. The previous government had banned such a transfer of knowledge; but the new revolutionary government had not made any decision about this. The issue became one for the crew itself to decide. The leader, being a teacher, felt that it was a good idea to transfer knowledge which is why the Earth authorities gained access to the ship and its engineering secrets.

Amanda expressed her anxiety about this development. "Do you really think we are ready to leap forward several centuries in terms of technical knowledge? Do we understand the dangers that you have learnt to deal with?"

I smiled. "I doubt very much you will learn much more than a few technical improvements to m-drive which will allow you to travel faster. I am sure that the most important things will be withheld."

Amanda became curious: "what are the most important things?" I decided to remain silent on this subject – at least until I was able to get to know her better.

The ship provided me with some essential supplies that I could not acquire on Earth; then it departed as suddenly as it had appeared. The scientists who had been aboard the ship worked furiously to develop new m-drive vehicles incorporating all that they had learnt. I was asked to inspect their work but, as I was no galactic ship engineer, I was not able to help them very much. The newly re-elected President asked to see me.

"Do you think we could visit your home planet with our ship without incurring the displeasure of your new revolutionary government?" I explained that there would be no problem with such a visit but that the crew would have to put themselves entirely under the supervision of the local tripedals.

"Without protection they would all be kropped." The President responded: "Surely, we could protect ourselves if we had some of your anti-krop powder?" I did not answer.

Amanda was becoming increasingly intimate with me. When we were alone and not being monitored by video cameras, she finally requested that I pump with her. She appeared to experience heightened sensations and I enjoyed her active participation. It was not until a few months of such mutually exciting activity that she popped the question that I had been expecting.

"You could tell me what the most important things are which your civilization withholds from us."

"Yes, I could: but then you would want me to tell you secrets which would be self-destructive."

"Of course, we would not want to behave in a self-destructive way. What nonsense!" Her insistence was touching but not convincing.

"Since you do not know what these secrets are about, how do you know what effect they could have?" I countered.

The resurgence of the kroppers came as a shock. I had not realised how many religious fundamentalists lived on Earth. They belong to a variety of belief systems but are characterized by the need to hold firm to fixed ideas. I know that as translators of religious texts, they have not learnt how to decipher the sophisticated codes so resort to absurd simplifications that miss the meaning completely. They appear incapable of living normal lives without holding views with a certainty that belies all reason and common sense and is contrary to the knowledge that all tripedals have learnt about the universe. They seem to require a focus for hatred: a scapegoat that fulfils their need to see evil incarnate on whom they can concentrate their desire to annihilate what they see as the source of all their troubles. They took over the government of neighboring countries and threatened war unless the President handed me over to their religious courts for trial. Amanda told me about these worrying developments.

"What charge would they bring against me?" I asked. She shrugged and said that the charge was irrelevant as the punishment was already decided. I realised that I had to make an important decision before it was too late.

The new m-drive ship was complete and ready for launch. The President announced that it would reach my home world in a week. I decided that I ought to be aboard before the kroppers could get to me. How to become a crewmember was not so straightforward. My celebrity and presence apparently reflected well on the President, so he did not like the idea of my leaving. Amanda certainly did not want me to go; but I said that I would really like her to come with me. So, we hatched a plan to get us both onto the ship.

I told her that the great secret lay in the development of the anti-krop powder. "This is our most advanced weapons system. Tell your President you have learnt this, and that the revolutionary government will use it against the new ship as part of the automated missile defense system. The ship will never reach its destination without my expertise in the ways of our world, and my willingness to communicate with the defense teams after launch."

The President reluctantly agreed to my returning with the ship, as a disastrous end to the trip would have effectively ended any hope for his administration to survive the following election. I then placed my final demand: refusing to go without Amanda.

The flight back was uneventful. Despite some teething trouble with the m-drive, we arrived back and were met by a lively team with plenty of powder cannons. I had communicated with them prior to landing. Needless to say, there was no automated missile defense system; I had simply made that up as an excuse to get back home. But when I described the developments on Earth to our revolutionary government's space exploration panel, they were very concerned by the resurgence of the fundamentalist kroppers. The monitoring of Earth broadcasts soon brought even worse news. The kroppers displaced the President in the election and declared war on all extra-terrestrials. They began building a fleet of m-drive ships and were arming them with nuclear bombs. We had discarded such ancient weaponry so long ago that only a few historians had any idea of their effect. When they described how devastating they could be, it was decided that a message would be sent demanding the disarming of such ships with the threat to destroy them if the demand were refused.

The problem with fundamentalists is they seem incapable of believing that they might not only be in the wrong, but it might also be idiotic to persist in what they regard as the only true path to follow. Their shipbuilding efforts were redoubled, and nuclear-armed ships were located ready for launch all over Earth. Reluctantly, the revolutionary government decided to powder their planet. A light dusting disabled all life forms temporarily. In the days whilst Earth's life literally stood still, our teams visited all the nuclear-armed ships and destroyed them. The stupidity of the kroppers was demonstrated when they then resumed nuclear bomb and m-drive shipbuilding in what they believed to be secret bunkers underground. Another warning was ignored. I asked Amanda what she thought we ought to do. Many of the previous Women's Council had befriended Amanda and she reflected their view that Earth needed to be powdered again. Unfortunately, the second powdering – when added to the powder from the initial injection – had unanticipated consequences. Most Earth life forms were incapable of surviving a double dusting, so their planet was effectively wiped out. I mourned the fact I would never see my children. Amanda, as the sole surviving human, became a celebrity and was elevated to the reinstated

Women's Panel after the revolutionary government fell in the wake of the Earth dusting catastrophe. I decided that it was time for my peaceful, final meeting with real krops.

I wheeled myself away from the station as the white sun was rising. A couple of duty bucks waved good-bye to me. The breeze caught my body as I rolled down towards the foothills. The landscape had a surreal quality, which I knew was a perceptual side effect of my mind assuming that it was about to be extinguished. Suddenly I heard the beating of their huge wings, the krops had spotted me. I came to a standstill, closed my eyes, and waited. The wing beating stopped, I took a deep breath and waited. And waited. And waited. I opened my eyes and saw a great krop on each side of me, just looking at me curiously. Then I received the biggest shock of my life. One krop opened its beak and spoke!

"You are the translator, aren't you?" I think all three of my mouths gawped in surprise. It continued: "Don't stand there looking amazed, we know that you can understand us if you are the translator."

I decided that I had better respond before they tore me to pieces. "I am a translator and I do understand you although I never knew you could speak."

The second krop appeared to make a comment that I could not make out. The first one cackled and said, "My colleague thinks that we should finish you off as we do not want tripedals to know how badly they underestimate us. But the moment we saw you trundle out this morning, our High Command issued an order that we will carry out. We want you to return to your people and persuade them to colonize the Earth."

I just stood there, disbelieving my own senses. I realised that if I had underestimated them, they clearly overestimated me. "You believe I have that much influence?" I asked. Both burst into the unpleasant cackling that I took to be the closest they could come to our more refined laughter response.

"We know you are a pathetic little teacher, but you can tell Amanda what we require, and she will do as you ask." And the two of them articulated their plan, checked that I had fully understood it, then flew off. Much to the surprise of the duty bucks, I rolled myself back to the station as the white sun began to set. After a total immersion fish bath, I decided to contact Amanda.

We met in the Central Pumping Station. She was delighted to see me. I told her that I had wanted to make my final krop meeting and she shook her head vigorously. "Don't you dare think such a thing! You are still young and the only one I can rely on to help me live here. Sometimes I feel I will go mad if I think about Earth. But then I know my life here is better than most and you are my anchor."

After we had retired to her private apartment, I explained how I had been confronted by the krops who wished us to keep quiet about their capacity for language and organization. Their plan was simple. They asserted that there was a balance in nature that we continuously attempted to destroy. Firstly, we had built the mountainside pumping station despite all their efforts to keep us to our coastal homes near the essential fish supply. Then the Earth ship had arrived and threatened to return to bring back more unruly bipeds: so, the krops had tried to prevent it by knocking down the ship. But we had gone ahead and established a disastrous contact with the distant planet that the krops believed had now brought about a different equilibrium. Their High Command had assessed the new situation and decided there was a way by which the new equilibrium could be properly established to prevent further catastrophes. I outlined their plan to Amanda and told her that they were relying on her influence within the Council to take it forward.

Amanda's powers turned out to be far greater than she and I realised. The Council regarded her with a mixture of deference and guilt. They deferred to her as the most experienced traveler within their tight-knit circle. And the guilt felt about the double dusting of her people translated itself into a willingness to go along with any plan she might have about Earth. She asserted that the vast numbers of corpses now littering the lands of her birth meant that extremely unpleasant micro-organisms would take over the planet which would, eventually, make it uninhabitable for future generations of tripedals. She countered the argument that we did not want to colonize the Earth by saying that this view might change so it was best to leave the option open. Her proposal to send flocks of krops to clean up the planet was reluctantly agreed, provided that there were no unacceptably high losses amongst those sent out to capture the krops.

The ships full of krops were taken across the galaxy soon after. The Council were astonished by the ease with which the krops were captured and came meekly to the aviary pens before take-off. There were no losses amongst the captors who reported a strange silence amongst the flocks who lined up and took themselves into the ships as if they were willing. Whilst the Earth-based flocks were clearing up the corpses, Amanda and I assessed the reports brought back by the transport ships. They described how Earth was far from dead. Humans might have been largely eradicated, but the seas were now teeming with fish. And contact had been made with a small group of surviving humans who, like us, did not appear to be affected by the anti-krop powder. Amanda then put into place the final part of the krop plan. She argued in the Council that we needed to establish a colony on Earth to assess the long-term effects of the double dusting. The Council felt morally bound to accede to any proposals she made concerning Earth. However, her enemies reacted in exactly the way we expected and wanted them to. They suggested that Amanda herself should return to Earth and no longer sit on the Council. To their surprise, she agreed provided that she could take protection against the krops and any tripedals who volunteered to accompany her.

So, we set off in a couple of ships and established the first pumping station near the sea so that the volunteer fisherwomen could provide us with food. The krops left us alone. The surviving humans approached us, and I discovered that their immunity to the dust had been inherited from their father – myself! And in my extreme old age I have watched the number of tripedals on Earth grow to such an extent that hundreds of pumping stations have had to be built to service their appetite for energy. Amanda is head of the Earth

Women's Council and no longer takes much notice of the Women's Council back home. The krops have re-established their role as disposers of old tripedals and I have filed a request to be allowed to meet them again at the disposal ground by the mountainside. Amanda asked me if I was sure that the krops would agree to consume me this time. I assured her that there was no doubt about it.

"Why are you so certain?" she enquired.

"Because the krops desire equilibrium. And, yet again, they are feeling threatened by a Women's Council decision to expand away from our coastal homes by building a mountain-side pumping station."

22

THE RINGS OF DIOMEDE

The Universe is a strange place. You can travel light years and find nothing of interest – just regular pulses of energy radiating from standard stars. But every now and again, it will throw up a unique event – never to be repeated.

My wife was present when the rings of Diomede cascaded. She was eighteen and on holiday with her parents when the first shower surprised the rural communities of this peaceful planet. The rings were so fine that they were scarcely visible from the ground. Since they did not interfere with communication and were almost unnoticed by ships that passed through them, astronomers had paid them little attention. We are not sure exactly why this thin string of dust became so active and started to spin out of control.

Jill told me how, on the first morning, it appeared that tiny fireworks were pricking the sky with specks of light that flashed for a second and then were gone. People watched the spectacular display as every colour imaginable illuminated the atmosphere high above throughout the day. By the evening, the display had settled to a red glow through which no stars were visible. It was not until the second morning that inexplicable happenings created a ripple of panic.

After her breakfast, Jill drank her usual large glass of water. It was only as she put the glass down that she noticed a faint glimmer around the rim. She ran to the tap to wash up and was amazed as the sparkle of the water threw out little explosions of blue light. The family joined others outside to compare experiences. It was there that they were awed by the sight that became famous. Televised footage was beamed all over the galaxy and scientists converged on the quiet planet to try to understand what we could all see. Like every other drop of water on Diomede, the sea radiated a blue light whose arcs and splinterings seemed to reflect the flashes of red overhead.

The event finished quite suddenly on the fourth day. It was as if a great switch had been thrown and the display ceased. All water resumed its normal placid form as if nothing had ever been disturbed. The rings had gone, but the scientists took up permanent positions in the community to study the phenomenon and its aftermath. And now, fifty years later, they have still come up with no credible theory. I know this for certain as I am about to retire as the head of the Diomede Research Institute. The cascade's withheld secrets have perplexed me for years and, as the frustrations have mounted, I know they have aged me. Jill, however, does not look a day over eighteen.

23

LOST IN TRANSLATION

Kyle often wondered what Jan had seen in him. She was the distinguished Professor of Galactic Languages in the University where he was the lowly foreman of the Corporation Refuse Collection service. It is true that he was quite a reasonable performer on the two-fingered Django Banjoleon, and she was a virtuoso on the hypermodern eight-octave flute. That is where they met – in the local amateur orchestra. But, apart from music, he would struggle to find what else they had in common.

Beneath the atemporal blanket cloud, our world was naturally protected from the warring factions who fought across the galaxy. Cut off from major trade routes, it was extremely rare that we had to host any unwelcome visitors. Without being able to converse directly with practitioners, this made Jan's mastery of the most obscure languages difficult. The almost impossible to detect deflections within the Vancoon click language meant that Jan was our planet's sole speaker of Vancoon when their war fleet overwhelmed all opposition in the so-called 'war to end all wars'. Kyle became genuinely afraid for his wife when she was called upon as the interpreter for the Vancoon military delegation that had flown through the atemporal cloud to meet with world leaders.

The first fear was the rumor that Vancoon displeasure with whoever they met often ended with them killing and eating their interlocutors – and that would include any interpreter! Secondly, the arrival of a full Vancoon fleet of heavily armed cruiser ships did not imply that the visit was merely for pleasure. Lastly, the appearance of a Vancoon admiral did not inspire comfortable viewing. Ten meters high with six tentacles, a head with three mouths and wearing what looked like a radioactive overcoat did not suggest that intimate friendship was the most likely outcome.

International regard for his wife leapt when she was watched across the world's vidscreens gesticulating and clicking with the monstrous admiral. The President of the World Council stood shivering some way off, listening to Jan's translation of the admiral's clicks. The President dared approach no nearer – probably fearful of becoming the admiral's lunch. Jan, on the other hand, showed no fear and even smiled at some of the clicks she received.

The President developed a stammer as he asked timidly what the Vancoon wanted. A lengthy click dialogue ensued during which Jan ignored the President and the watching vidscreens as she devoted herself to an intense conversation with the giant above her.

The President called out; 'what is he asking for?'

Jan waved him away: "Be quiet, I need to concentrate."

The admiral boomed a peculiar sound from his abdomen and three Vancoon members of his crew joined him in response. The President and his entourage started backing away, concerned that this larger group of warriors was about to attack. But Jan stood her ground and kept clicking. The four Vancoons stopped to attend to what she was saying. Then they clicked together in a high velocity rat-a-tat-a-tat-a-tat conversation that Jan later admitted to Kyle that she had trouble in following. But the result was a huge relief to the officials and met with an audible cheer around the world as vidscreen watchers saw the monsters slowly move back into the lead battle cruiser. They took off leaving Jan to explain what had been said.

Jan faced the vidscreen and announced: "The Vancoon demands are simple. They expect immediate implementation, or the admiral and his party will return to have them enforced."

Her words were recorded and set out as the non-negotiable top priority of every political party for the coming year.

"Our refuse collectors are to be paid double; our interpretation services are to receive three times their current funding; and all musicians at any level of competence are to receive a basic State subsidy for every week they play, practice or perform music."

24

FREELANCE

He had enjoyed a good life. It is true that he had never earned much money and had never found the right woman with whom he could share his passion for music. But he still performed on the same violin that had been presented to him by Hippolyte the impressive President of South American Bank Corporation after he had won the Amazon competition when he was only sixteen. It was a valuable fiddle that he always kept with him: in his bedroom, when in transit, on the toilet ... he never let it out of his reach.

He remembered his plane trip from Brussels to Rio all those years ago. It was the first of many flights: he had seen concert halls in China, America, Russia, India, Australia, Japan. He even kept the fiddle to hand when on hunting trips where he used a different type of bow with arrows. He recalled the exciting trip to Arcadia, the exhausting one up the rocky Mount Erymanthus and even frightening nights stalking the huge birds in the Stymphalian marshes. He had amassed hundreds of trophies as well as thousands of airmiles and managed, despite many offers, to avoid the one great fear that he had had since childhood. He had never been on a boat.

His fear of the sea was so great that he even turned down a lucrative contract to play on one of the great ocean liners. What was worse was the offer had been made to a small group of musician friends with whom he would have loved to play. But he had made a lame excuse about prior engagements that, unfortunately, were becoming less common as he got older. Younger players were preferred by the agents who allocated gigs. They were aware that his age meant he would be retired or dead whilst some of the new graduates still had years of playing before them. Their investment always looked at the long-term.

When the crash occurred, it was unfortunate that the injury he sustained required surgery. The violin remained safe inside its hard-shell case, but his health insurance company squirmed out of its commitment to cover his treatment. He wondered why he had even bothered to pay the premium. But he had no choice but to have the operation. Recovery took a couple of months. Without work, freelancers like him had no income. By the time he was reunited with his instrument (it had been left in his brother's locked safe) he was desperate for work.

He called his agent who explained that most of the orchestral work had been farmed out to other freelancers. But there were some summer gigs coming up on the Mediterranean.

"You would have to get yourself down there, and there's no travel expenses. But the pay isn't bad. Are you interested?"

He felt he had no choice so, in days, he had flown down to Greece where the engagements had been arranged. He felt panic and horror when he saw that the music was to be performed on the deck of a ship. The trepidation with which he stepped onto the gang plank was noticed by one of the other performers.

"There's nothing to be frightened about," the woman who was carrying a violin case strapped on her back, said in a quiet French accent.

He smiled at her attempt at reassurance but decided to keep his eyes fixed well away from the side handrails. He just glared straight ahead and said:

"Do you know where we will be performing?"

"I think it will be on the upper deck. Then, when everyone has eaten, we will go below and play in what they call the ballroom although it is nothing more than a narrow dance floor."

She smiled at him and announced: "My name is Charonne."

"Thank you, Charonne. I am Hercule," he replied. He assumed she had experience on this boat or something similar. "I'll follow you if you know the way."

They climbed the wooden steps on what he suspected was quite an old boat. There were tiny shelves fixed against the walls upon which ornaments were displayed. He could not help noticing that they were shown higgledy-piggledy with no attempt to place similar articles beside one another. His impression was that the owners were more interested in appearance than content. Perhaps they felt the same about the music.

Once on the upper deck, he felt dizzy as he could not avoid seeing the sea. They were at anchor, so the gentle rocking motion was only caused by disturbance from passing craft. He placed himself firmly in his seat and focused all his attention on the music stand that he found he was sharing with his French colleague.

"Are you alright?" she asked.

"I am sure I'll be fine once we are playing."

The leader/conductor was already standing at the front surveying his tiny chamber orchestra: eight violins, four violas, four cellos and a double bass.

"Let's play Bach!" he announced in a posh English accent.

It seemed that the players had never played together. But, as professionals, they did a reasonable job of the Bach suites. The sound of the guests talking below did not disturb them: but the occasional lurching of the boat when a large ship passed by found him holding onto his chair instead of playing. His colleague pretended not to notice and just played a little louder when he had these occasional lapses.

Mozart divertimenti and the inevitable Eine Kleine Nachtmusik followed Bach, and the ensemble improved as they grew accustomed to each other and the unusual surroundings. There was even a moment when he completely forgot about being on the water as he immersed himself in the music.

"We have a break now," Charonne announced.

Hercule carefully laid his violin back into its case and closed the lid.

"Can we spend it back on dry land?" he asked.

Charonne looked puzzled. She pointed to the stern of the boat, and he was seized with fright. The harbor was just visible on the horizon: they had sailed while he had been concentrating on Mozart.

"We play for them to dance whilst we are at sea at night. We are meant to conjure up a few romantic hours in the darkness. The boat lands before the sun rises. Didn't you have this explained to you by your agent?"

Hercule felt himself shaking. He took deep breaths but, somehow, this did not settle his nerves. Charonne looked worried at how he was failing to cope with the news.

"Perhaps it would be better if you could just lie down for a while until it is time to play again. Come with me. There is a cabin set aside for emergencies."

He picked up his violin and hugged it to his chest. As he staggered after her, he felt as if he was hanging on to the case as if it was a life buoy preventing him from drowning. They reached the cabin door which was swinging open and shut with the motion of the boat. Somehow, he did not find that reassuring but walked into the little room which seemed more like a prison cell than a place of escape.

"Just lie down on the bunk," Charonne said. "It should settle you. Tell me, do you want anything to eat?" He shook his head.

"Well, I need to eat. I will not be long, and I'll bring you back something to drink."

And, in an instant, she was gone. Hercule was sitting on the bunk still clasping his violin case. He froze. He could not move. He knew she had told him to lie down but his body just refused to relax back onto the bunk. It was as if the idea of lying back was a movement that would not stop when he reached the bed. His imagination had him sinking through the cabin floor, into the ship's hold, passing through the keel and into the cold sea that was patiently waiting for him. "My violin will keep me afloat," he said out loud in English. And still, he did not move.

He was still there when Charonne returned with a hot drink.

"Let me hold your violin so you can drink this up," she said.

But he did not budge. She frowned. "I won't hurt your violin, Hercule. I just think you really do need a hot drink."

He nodded and, very gingerly, held out the violin case so that he could take the mug of tea from Charonne. Sipping it seemed to relax him a little although he kept his gaze fixed upon his violin.

As Hercule was Belgian and Charonne was French, it was logical to converse in French. But perhaps because the conductor spoke to everyone in English, they kept to the language that all the musicians seemed to understand.

"Where is your violin?" he asked.

"I've left it on the chair ready for the dance."

"Are you happy to leave a valuable violin unattended?" He was genuinely shocked at the thought.

Charonne laughed. "The violin I carry around for these gigs is a cheap factory instrument. I think I picked it up for a few euros when a local shop was clearing out stock they had bought from China. My good violin is safely at home."

Hercule gave a little start of surprise. He had never thought of doing what she had achieved in terms of guarding his beloved instrument by simply replacing it with a cheap one when on unimportant tours like this one. He made a mental note: if he ever managed to survive this experience on water, he would invest a tiny sum for a modern plastic violin.

"Anyway, it's nearly time to play again," Charonne announced and made for the cabin door when the boat made a sudden lurch. Hercule found himself on the floor with Charonne on top of him with his violin case jammed between them. Charonne thought nothing of this unexpected incident but was very concerned when she found Hercule hyperventilating underneath her and his violin.

She carefully placed the violin on the bunk and tried to help Hercule back onto his feet. But he felt his legs had turned into uncontrollable, quivering trouser-filled blancmange. They were incapable of supporting his body.

"Just give me a moment," he appealed to Charonne.

"All right. But if we don't play, they don't pay," she intoned this well-rehearsed epigram.

The thought of coming this far and then not getting the fee brought a hot flush to Hercule's cheeks and blood pumping through his deflated legs. He staggered to his feet, grasped his violin, and followed Charonne out of the cabin. The dance floor was full of guests chatting. They showed no sign of wanting to dance until their conductor/leader, seemingly suddenly aware that most of the players were French, shouted: "Allons-y. Danse numéro un!"

Hercule made a mental note that this was another French

musician. Perhaps he was the only Belgian here. Maybe everyone else was from Paris and had played together for years. But
then he remembered how disjointed the first Bach suite had
sounded and concluded that none of them probably knew
each other until now.

They began playing a piece that Hercule had never seen,
and after a few nondescript bars, he hoped he would never
see again. But the guests had started to arrange themselves in
couples and were dancing nonchalantly to the music. So, the
ensemble repeated the piece a few times before moving on to
"numéro deux"

Charonne did not appear to mind the boredom of the music they were required to play. They were technically simple
enough for amateurs to perform reasonably well so required
no rehearsal, no attention to detail and no concern with strict
accuracy. Nonetheless, as professionals no one was making
any mistakes and the dancers seemed content with what was
being presented to them.

The evening was becoming warm, and the strings were becoming flat. But no one seemed to care. One woman fainted
and was carried off the dance floor, but no one seemed to
notice. One of the violists stopped playing as one of her
strings broke, but the musicians continued without worrying
about that. Finally, the conductor put down his violin and
walked away which signaled a twenty-minute interval when
the players could grab a drink.

Charonne led Hercule to the bar where the musicians
were permitted a single complementary drink – "preferably
water" they were informed by the barman. Holding a glass of

lukewarm water, Hercule made his way across the deck, away from the bar, and found himself pressed up against the guard-rail on the other side of the boat. He had lost Charonne in the crush but was holding the glass in one hand and his violin case in the other when he found himself looking over the rail without having a hand to steady himself. For a moment, he imagined that the rail would not be sturdy enough to prevent him from being plunged into the sea below. Instinctively, he dropped the glass, and it tumbled over the side. Grabbing the rail with his free hand, he watched aghast as the glass ricocheted its way down the side of the boat and disappeared beneath the waves. He stared at the way the water was being divided by the boat's hull, driving forward, and creating a regular wave pattern that repeated itself again and again. He was fascinated by the intricate patterns being made as the waves intercepted one another further behind where he was standing. Suddenly Charonne was beside him.

"There you are! I thought you had got lost."

"No, but I lost a glass of water over the side," he admitted sheepishly.

"I'd keep that quiet if I were you," she suggested. "They would think nothing of charging you for the glass and taking it off your fee!"

"I wonder how much they would charge if we bought a glass of beer or wine."

"Let's find out," Charonne said mischievously.

She walked up to the barman and enquired the price of various alcoholic beverages. He spent some time going through the sums he assumed he would be collecting from the beleaguered musicians, all desperate with thirst. But after a couple of minutes, she just explained to him. "Ah! Quelle domage! C'est beaucoup trop cher pour les musiciens," and she walked away.

One of the guests overheard this exchange and intervened. As guests could consume as much alcohol as they wanted without paying, he gallantly offered Charonne a free glass of beer that he had just been handed by the barman. She smiled, thanked the kind man, and shared the drink with Hercule who looked as if he really needed it.

The boat ploughed on its way and the music accompanied the dancers who began to flag after a couple of hours. Hercule realised that it was getting close to the end of the trip. He assumed that the guests would be deposited back at the port, and they would, finally, be allowed to disembark and escape from the lurching waves. He joined Charonne in carefully re-placing his violin in its case as the dancers gathered to leave the boat. Charonne was watching them attentively as if awaiting any unhappiness at the disembarkation arrangements.

"What's the problem?" he asked. "Why are you watching that lot so closely?"

"Some might not like the destination. We have had people rebelling at the prospect of being landed here."

"Are we not back at the original port?" he asked.

Charonne shook her head. "No, this lot are on a one-way trip. There is no return booked for any of them."

And within ten minutes, the dancers had all left and filed through the strange archway decorated with the statue of a three-headed dog. Some of the musicians joined them.

"Do we have to disembark here?" Hercule enquired.

"Not this time," Charonne replied. "We can sleep in the bunk, and we'll be returned to our point of departure. Will you be okay with that?"

Hercule looked at where the dancers had walked up the quay and were already disappearing into the gloom. Despite his fear, he instinctively knew that he was not destined to conclude this trip on this land.

"Let's get back," he responded. "I've still a lot of music to play before this final journey."

25

ANGELA

Angela is a well-educated scientist who sacrificed her career for her husband's vocation. Brian knew Angela from the church: their families were regular attenders, so they were thrown together throughout their teens. When Angela finished her physics degree and returned to the town, Brian successfully wooed the only girl he had ever wanted. He became the local vicar with Angela as a devoted vicar's wife.

Sometimes I think I can hear Brian's evangelical voice when Angela speaks. I cannot quite understand how this highly qualified scientist accustomed to logical thinking can talk about Biblical miracles as "fact". My puzzlement about virgin birth is answered by a strange peroration about parthenogenesis (Angela the scientist) or an assertion concerning how God can "break into" our regular life as He is omnipotent, omniscient, omnipresent, and invisible. "Invisibility is useful in avoiding interrogation," I counter, much to Brian's annoyance.

I met Angela and Brian in the street in the afternoon. They asserted that they had experienced a miracle. "We had taken a walk through the woods and as we emerged, we saw a man approaching the woods from the adjoining field. We couldn't see his face. But we watched him discarding his cloak and slowly floated to the ground as if completing a flight."

"Yes," Brian interjected. "He was gliding."

"We know we were witnessing an angel!"

"How do you figure that?" I asked.

"Because the cloak was covering a wing!"

"How far away was this figure?"

They looked at one another and admitted that the next field was about a kilometer away. "But this was no vision. We could see him as clearly as we see you now."

"You don't think that what looked like a wing was the lining of his cloak. And as the sun was quite hot this afternoon, the air can shimmer over the field which could generate the appearance of floating."

Brian was finding it hard to hide his frustration with me. "You are just an unbeliever who will always try to find an explanation that obscures the reality of divine intervention."

"Science describes much," Angela said. "But it fails to grasp how events are connected when there seems to be no rational explanation. I doubt if any miracle, however clear, would be accepted by you as anything other than a physical event whose cause was as yet uncertain."

"On the other hand," I countered, "you are only too quick

to ascribe supernatural intervention as the cause of anything extraordinary that you might expect from the Biblical deity about whom you read every day in church."

Angela and Brian walked off, shaking their heads at my skeptical response to what they had witnessed in the field. I waited until they had turned the corner before vowing to myself to be far more circumspect in future as I adjusted my wing.

26

KEEPING MUM

Sometimes, someone you think you know well can surprise you. My mum waited until I was quite old before she sprung her surprise. She and my dad had lived in their anonymous semi-detached house ever since I was born. The street was round the corner from my school where I did quite well in science (I was always rubbish at writing). My dad encouraged me to study computer science as he said he had always found work as a computer technician. He had met my mum whilst at college where she was on the same course. And there were times that she helped me with my problems: but she tended to leave difficult questions for my dad when he got home from work.

The town where we lived, Middleton, (not its real name) had few redeeming features. I asked my mum why they had chosen to set up home here.

She said: "Darling, I really do value my privacy. And when we moved here, it was all we could afford at the time."

As an only child, I felt close to my parents. I liked the fact that there was a set routine to the day with my mum constantly at home and my dad leaving for work at seven thirty and returning without fail at six o'clock. I remember that there were odd times when my mum would disappear for a couple of days and my dad would take those days off. I would ask her where she had been. And she would invariably answer "up to town to see about a few things."

What was my mum known for in our street? She liked to cook and contributed cakes to the local fair where food was sold to support the school or hospital. Neighbors liked to buy what she had made as they said she had a flair for kitchen work; and she would agree that this was her main talent. When I was very young, she would walk me to school and chat with the other mums about the problems of bringing up youngsters on a restricted budget, the inclemency of the weather, and gossip concerning women on the next street.

One year my dad announced we were going abroad for a holiday to Genevieve (not its real name). We had never left the country before, so I was excited. The flight found me glued to the window watching the landscape far below until it disappeared beneath cloud. We stayed in a hotel that was so plush that I could not even hear my own footsteps in the carpet. Walking down a side street the next day, we went into a little bank to withdraw money. We were the only customers and my mum spoke to the clerk behind the counter in a foreign language. As we left, she said to me "I call this place the Belch bank". I thought this was very funny. I burped and my dad laughed. But my mum shook her head and said, "one day you will appreciate Belch."

I was forty when my mum sprung her surprise. My dad had just retired, and they were talking about moving house. My wife and I lived only a few doors away and our children loved to play in their grandparents' garden. My dad said they would not go far away as they wanted to stay close to us and see the kids whenever they could. But they wanted a quieter home as they were finding the street quite noisy. I asked if I could help and if they had enough money to afford a place in the country.

My dad shook his head and said: "It seems your mum has a little nest egg so we should be okay."

Later that day my mum took me aside. "I've not told you about my little nest egg before and even your dad does not really know much about it. But I think you ought to know about it now."

What she told me was such a shock that I have never really recovered. In fact, the reason I am writing this note to you all is to try to gain some advice about what I should do. Apparently, my mum was no ordinary computer technician student when she met my dad. She had already created the program that successfully extracted tiny amounts that existed when currency was exchanged between banks. The amounts were so infinitesimally small that no one had noticed their disappearance. For every few hundred thousand transactions, a cent was built up in one of her accounts. She had implanted her program in all banks throughout the world and had been earning an illegal billion dollars every year. She bought a private bank into which all her ill-gotten gains were deposited. She called it BELCH, short for the Bank for the Extraction of Loose Change. She was, by some considerable margin, the wealthiest person on the planet and, by the purchase of shares through a network of dummy investment corporations, owned a majority shareholding in many of the world's best-known companies. However, she had taken steps from the earliest days to ensure that her anonymity was protected. In fact, she said that I was the only person other than her accountant in BELCH to know of the extent of her riches. "Now I am retiring," she concluded; "you need to know as you are now the owner of BELCH and, therefore, the owner of all the companies in which I have invested."

My parents now live happily in a pleasant bungalow not far from Middleton (not its real name). I have continued to work as a computer technician without revealing our family secret. My multi-national fizzy-drink employer, Alac O'coc (not its real name), knows nothing of my immense wealth and I am careful not to make any unusually expensive purchases. To my knowledge, my mum's program is still piling billions of dollars into the BELCH accounts every year. The accountants keep buying more and more of the world's shares: I suspect that I own Alac O'coc as well as its main competitor, Pispe (not its real name). I have said nothing to my wife and children. However, I am beginning to wonder whether I might be able to do something positive with all these riches: but without compromising the family's reputation for honesty and hard work. Has anyone any suggestions?

Ray Kohn (not my real name?)

27

THE CUBE

Being a 23rd century chronicler is a privilege. I am well aware of the duties and responsibilities that such a position holds. So, if you are reading this in the 24th or 25th centuries, please take into account the circumstances in which I write before passing judgement upon my objectivity (however you may be defining that in your era).

We think of the Cube as the culmination of our planet's technology. In the 22nd century, its construction in Earth orbit was, by all accounts, the most ambitious project undertaken in collaboration between the many competing agencies, nations, and power holders. Its proportions, over 200 kilometers cubed, was intended to recognize that those leaving our planet would find it difficult to live side by side. So vast areas were set aside for each grouping on the understanding that they did not need to meet on any regular basis and could coexist in their self-sufficient regions.

The broad scientific view by the end of the 21st century was that the planet was unlikely to survive in a habitable state for very much longer. The Cube was created, officially, "to preserve the human race beyond life on Earth". Competition to reserve places on the construction was intense; but, in truth, only those with power, money, and influence could ever hope to get on board. Our great grandparents who remained were told to make the best of the land that was left, despite the destruction that had been wrought during the early 21st century wars.

We have an account of the cube's departure from the contemporary chronicler whose words I would not even attempt to surpass:

The great ship, as large as a planet, slowly moved away from Earth. Its lights illuminated all of Brazil and surrounding lands for over a week. As it picked up velocity, messages beamed back to us took on a distinctly sneering quality. Leah, who managed the communication system based in Auckland, recorded the final message from the Cube. She reported that it was best read only by adults who thought it worth knowing what those in charge of the Cube's Regions thought of "the weaklings left on the doomed planet".

In the decades after the departure of the Cube, Earth acquired a different hue. Areas previously cultivated for meat production became overgrown as vegetable and fruit consumption became the norm. Some fishing was retained but human appetites altered without any apparent orders from above. By the end of the 22nd century, the anticipated self-destruction of our planet became a subject of interest, but not of news. Far more attention was being paid to how the profusion of organisms seemed to have become central to the development of life on Earth. Leah's children, for example, became famous for their study of how bacterial evolution accelerated in collaboration with mycelia, and my own parents made a living by growing a vast variety of mushrooms.

Although communication with those in the Cube was only sporadic, it became clear to us that those on board could not help coming into conflict with one another. It seems that the initial issue was to do with shared access to the farming areas. There had been an agreement before the Cube's launch that weapons would not be needed on board as there would be no conflict: but it is also undoubtedly true that this agreement was systematically broken by those in charge of every Region. We may never know exactly how the conflict that destroyed the Region numbered S17 to W510, but we could observe the effect on even the most basic telescopes. The top quarter on the right of the Cube had disintegrated and the entire construction started to spin out of control. Having taken up a position orbiting just beyond Jupiter, their trajectory away from the giant planet took them irrevocably into the path of Saturn which, to coin a classical image, literally ate them up.

Last year one of our leaders, the Co-operator Ding Luo, asked if anyone would be interested in exploring the near planets to see if there were alternative life forms that might have developed underground. She made a good case that mycelia could survive the extreme conditions on both Mars and Venus. This week, she reported to me for the Chronicle that no one wanted to be involved.

28

QUIZ

Wilson hated it when he was pushed into doing something he instinctively disliked. But his wife had become a keen quizzer, often in demand by others to join their team with all-round knowledge of things Wilson regarded as irrelevant.

The evening began. They sat awaiting the questions to which they had to give immediate verbal replies. The other teams did not seem to be doing very well so when it came to their turn, his wife was excited with the prospect of an easy win.

"Please complete the following saying.

"A bird in the hand is worth ...

"Wilson answered instantly ... "very little."

His wife glared at him, but the invited audience clapped enthusiastically and laughed at Wilson's joke. The compere listened to instructions passed to him through his earpiece and, to the obvious annoyance of the other teams, announced:

"That was not the reply I have written here: but it has been judged as better than the one we hold.

The other teams were provided with further easy questions until it came to Wilson's turn again.

"Too many cooks spoil ..."

"...weight watchers!"

Audience applause exasperated the competitive teams although some had begun to participate in Wilson's quiet derision of the exercise. His wife just sat back and said: "I think you had better answer all the quotations this evening." Some replies seemed to reflect Wilson's background as a scientist which his wife suspected would not be appreciated by the audience. But as they were seated in a university lecture theatre, she was wrong because most of those watching them were undergraduates.

"A stitch in time ..."

".. is a superstring" brought the house down although neither his wife nor the compere understood the joke.

"Every cloud has a silver ...

"...iodide lining for rainmaking" drew applause from the meteorologists.

"A rolling stone..."

"... accelerates downhill."

The lights dimmed and the compere became very serious. "I am going to give you famous sayings to which you need to provide an explanation. Do you understand?" Wilson's wife nodded although he was unsure what was meant to happen.

"OK. Here is your first one. Your days are numbered..."

"... but less so in February," Wilson responded instantly.

"I'm afraid that that does not explain the saying," the compere intoned. "I'll throw it open to the other teams." But much to the compere's annoyance, the other teams said they liked Wilson's take on the saying and thought it illustrated the meaning perfectly.

One of the other team captains shouted out to Wilson, "Curiosity killed the cat…"

Wilson called back: "I think the verdict is expected today!"

The audience were in fits and the compere was becoming irate at his inability to control proceedings.

"Cloak and dagger" one of the other team captains cried out.

"… to cut a rough buttonhole" Wilson shouted back.

"That's enough!" the compere insisted. "Let's get back to the game…" to which Wilson replied, "I don't think that is an appropriate saying for family entertainment."

The audience was in stitches of laughter, and even his wife had tears running down her cheeks at her husband's unexpected wit.

"A journey of a thousand miles begins with a …"

"… car hire?"

"A man after my own heart …"

"… that's my cardiac surgeon!"

The compere just gave up at this point and let the opposition captains set Wilson the questions.

"A picture is worth a thousand …"

"… dollars if it's an original."

"Absence makes the heart grow…

"… forgetful?"

"Beauty is only skin…"

"… shaped?"

"Butter wouldn't melt in his mouth…"

"..because he died yesterday."

But Wilson was getting bored and clearly wanted to finish the evening. He looked to his wife for a lead, and she said:

"A fate worse than…"

"…a quiz night."

And they all went home.

29

ANGELIC HOST

It is extremely annoying when you go in for a service and the job is not carried out. Despite protestations to the contrary that the work had been completed to the required standard, actions speak louder than words.

I have flown for enough years to know if a wing has been properly mended. I was carrying out a quick tour when I came down with a bump. The woman I nearly knocked over screamed and within a minute she had half a dozen men running to her assistance. I tried to explain to her that my landing on her was an accident, but she would not listen. She kept shouting at me and pointing to my shoulder where the damaged wing was protruding.

It was abundantly clear to me that unless I acted promptly, it would be more than my wing that was torn. I had never used the time transformation facility, but this was an emergency. The mob seemed to me to have frozen in time although I knew that this was just an illusion. Brushing past the men I was tempted to give the meanest looking one a punch on the nose, but I thought better of it and just ran on leaving them perplexed as to how the stranger had disappeared.

My priority was to get the wing mended. But I was unsure how to go about this without even knowing where I had landed. The countryside around here was green and peaceful but devoid of passers-by who might have been able to show me where I could get at least a temporary fix.

On the hill at the top of the road, there was a large poster board. Perhaps that might give me a clue as to where I should go. I walked slowly up the hill, annoyed at not being able to flit through the air as usual. By the time I had reached the top, I was feeling tired and out-of-breath. Perhaps my condition, combined with the aggravation caused by the useless engineering crew to whom I am attached for wing maintenance, explained my non-angelic reaction to what I saw.

The picture of the man demanding my vote at the forthcoming presidential election in no way resembled those we had been shown at angel school in the lessons about dictators responsible for the death of millions. However, there was something about his demeanor that told me that he would soon join them in our next seminar as a more up-to-date example. I was so angry just at the sight of his smug face that I fired a tiny posterior thunderbolt that destroyed the posterboard in a flash.

I looked around to see if anyone had witnessed this unforgiveable act of vandalism. We were taught the importance of non-interference from our very first days at school. Humans, we are told, are responsible for their own fates. The contrary opinion held by the 'cetacean team' whom I must admit I respected although, clearly, they did not have sanctification from on high, was that we should intervene for the sake of the truly innocent. They had a three-dimensional image of Moby Dick that they projected onto the wall whenever we had this discussion. Their belief was that the only creatures that held value in these terms were whales and dolphins. Therefore, intervention on their behalf was an angelic duty. The problem that they had in arguments at school was that once intervention was seen as permissible in one case, others were sure to follow. So, our teachers explained that this was the 'slippery slope' doctrine which officially ruled out intervention and the very highest authority proclaimed that it would never be sanctioned.

I was pondering about this old argument as I walked on down the hill. I know I have an unfortunate habit of talking to myself. "Stop mumbling!" I was told throughout my childhood, but it is difficult to prevent yourself doing something that is part of your very makeup.

"Perhaps the will to intervene is itself part of some angels' makeup," I said to myself.

"What did you say?"

I was startled by this voice. A woman on a bicycle had been riding down the hill and came alongside me just as I was muttering.

"Oh. Sorry. I didn't see you. I was just talking to myself."

"Did you see the posterboard? Someone has a real attitude daring to destroy one of his posters. If any of his supporters saw the culprit, they would beat him up like they've done to other opponents in the city. It wasn't you, was it?" she asked coyly. She knew very well it was me, but I thought it would be amusing to play innocent.

"Why? Are you going to beat me up," I replied.

She laughed. "Look back up there. You'll see that I followed up your demolition by setting fire to the wreckage. My friends and I would do anything to see that vile man beaten in the election. But we know that will never happen as he always wins. He has those mad supporters who thinks he is some kind of god – and that includes powerful people who run the media here."

I nodded as if I knew what she was talking about.

"You aren't from around here, are you?" she asked.

"No. Actually, you might be able to help me. I'm looking for someone who can do some running repairs."

"What sort of repairs?"

"If I had an injured pet, where would I go if it were an injured bird with a damaged wing?"

"You would need a vet. And guess what? I am a veterinary surgeon with my own practice. So, if you show me your bird, I am sure I can help."

I looked at the young woman. Could I trust her with the sight of my wing? She would know that I was certainly not from "around here". But, there again, what choice did I have? Perhaps I could erase some part of her memory. I had heard that some colleagues had achieved this, but I had never tried it. With no one else in sight, I pulled off my overall and revealed my injury.

"Well, I never!" she exclaimed. "So, you are the pet!" and

she burst out laughing. Eventually, she calmed down and started a professional inspection of my wing.

"I can sort this out," she announced. "But I want you to do something for me as payment."

"Sorry. I have no money."

"I don't want money. I want you to do something instead."

"How quick can you repair the wing?"

She reached into her saddlebag and pulled out what looked like a long comb. "Stand still," she demanded. I waited for her to hold me by my shoulder, but she went straight for the wing with her comb. After a minute of feather combing, the wing suddenly jumped by itself, then settled down into its natural position."

"That should work," she said. "You'll find it will function fine now."

I extended both wings and found take-off very easy. A quick circle around and I returned beside my saviour.

"I want to thank you very much. Tell me what I can do for you."

"You know the man whose picture you destroyed. I want you to somehow discover what horrible things he is planning so we can prepare our defenses."

I wondered whether this would break the non-interference rule. If this politician had no notion of who I was and never learnt how his enemies discovered his secrets, I couldn't see how I could be admonished as it would all seem to happen as if I'd not been there.

"Where will I find him? And how will I find you afterwards?"

The vet cyclist pulled out a notepad from her bag and scribbled instructions for me.

"I trust you to carry out what you promised," she said as I took off on my way to where she had instructed me to fly.

The capital was easy to find. Smoke and exhaust fumes filled the atmosphere for hundreds of kilometers in all directions. I surveyed the city and quickly identified where the leader was installed. It seems that the more odious the leader, the more layers of physical protection are built around him. I landed on a balcony that I calculated would bring me near what they call "the seat of power" (I never understood what a chair had to do with power). Pushing open the bay window I found myself in an empty room with a large table upon which were several heavily marked maps. Curious, I started studying them.

Suddenly, the door at the other end of the room opened and half a dozen men marched in accompanied by the leader. They could not see me as I had used an aspect of the time transformation facility that made their perception of me impossible without angelic spectacles. The men were pointing at the maps and the leader was shouting about how they needed to be more precise about where the attacks should be aimed.

"Through the sea," one replied. And the others all nodded in agreement.

"How many of our men would die?" another asked. The leader scowled at him as if it was an irrelevant question.

"The explosions offshore when the fighting begins will bring us lots of fish floating to our table," one laughed.

It was only at that moment that I realised the men were being watched by the entire cetacean team – all wearing angelic spectacles and looking straight at me!

"What are you doing here?" one asked me.

"Never mind me: what are you lot doing here?"

"Today, we are the angelic host!"

"So, are you here to stop me interfering?

"Stop asking questions and answer ours."

"I've promised to report this man's plans to his opponents. But otherwise, I won't interfere, I promise you. Why? What are you doing here?"

"You can go and do your report," the team leader replied, "and you can tell them that the heart attack that is about to kill this leader has been ordered by Moby Dick."

An image of the giant whale flashed up onto the wall behind the leader. All his people saw it just as their boss clasped his chest and collapsed. The image disappeared and so did the cetacean team.

It only took me five minutes to fly to where my vet saviour had cycled home. I reported that the leader's death, which would be reported next day, had nothing to do with me. She smiled, nodded but clearly did not believe me. Unfortunately, no one up here believes me either because the cetacean team deny all knowledge of what happened. On the other hand, the repair to my shoulder by a woman who was a major opponent of the dead leader is well recorded. This has set me up as the prime suspect in the upcoming anti-interference trial. I've even had my wings clipped! The useless wing engineering team have a lot to answer for!

30

HIGH RISE

She was proud to live in the luxury apartment at the top of the world's tallest building. When she looked out across the city, she could see the grey air conditioning units pumping away silently on the roofs of buildings far below. Beyond the irregularly packed city blocks, she could glimpse a slender stretch of ocean glimmering beneath the hazy horizon.

She had become accustomed to the movement of the Tower upon which she was perched: the slight waves across the bath as the water never seemed to be able to rest, the daily routine of straightening the paintings that she had hung meticulously across the dining room wall, her feigned ignoring of the way that the mock chandelier seemed to rock in time with her breathing.

Sajid, her former boyfriend, told her that he felt dizzy in the apartment. She told herself that they had to split up because he was unable to survive at the heights at which she lived. He had been unkind after abruptly walking out of the party where she and her female friends had been comparing notes on the benefits of their various homes. She challenged him as to why he had been so rude, and he responded by pointing out that most of them only owned their respective homes because of the wealth of the families into which they had been born. She told him that he was jealous because his family were not as rich as hers, and he had walked out without another word.

Of course, she knew that Sajid was right in observing that her father's company was very profitable. She did not understand how he had made so much money. It had something to do with trading items of value between continents and, as a result, she rarely saw her father. He seemed to spend more time in South America and Asia than at home; but she could not complain about the financially limitless trust fund that he had set up for her. Her brother had been chosen to oversee the American arm of the company, so she only ever saw him on big family occasions like her father's sixtieth birthday party.

The party had been in London: so, she had flown to Heathrow and taken a taxi to the five-star hotel selected to hold the party. Her room was acceptable; but nowhere near what she was used to in her own apartment. 'Never mind', she thought. 'One must make allowances when traveling. Not everywhere can reach the standards that our family sets itself.'

She had taken a great deal of trouble in selecting clothes

appropriate for the occasion. She had travelled to Tokyo for the pure silk kimono and to her favorite milliner in New York for the rhinestone headband decorated with diamonds. The crystal shoes had been made especially for her in Paris and the antique brooch holding together the font of her kimono had been the most prized piece of jewelry owned by her mother before she died. Her father had complimented her finery, but she was piqued at her brother ignoring her for most of the evening.

When she got back to her apartment, she was greeted with the usual unwanted batch of begging letters. Just because she was rich did not mean that she was required to dispense funds to those whom she believed did not usually deserve support. She made exceptions for applicants who bothered to offer her something in return. For example, she liked seeing her name featured at the start and the end of a film that she could claim to have commissioned. She was proud that her father had noticed her pet project when the art gallery near the Tower took her family's name after she donated a few hundred thousand dollars for essential building work. At the party, the only words that her brother had spoken to her were "what good comes from wasting money on a load of paintings?"

She despised her brother and called him a philistine as he also had no appreciation of her own substantial artistic talents. She had one of her north-facing rooms kitted out so that she could create fine art which she knew would be appreciated long after she had died. She asserted they were too "far ahead of their time" for even her own gallery to display to a contemporary audience. So, they were carefully wrapped and stacked in one of the other apartments that she rented especially for artistic storage.

She was puzzled when a police inspector called, with a team of officers, and demanded to inspect the arts store. They claimed that "contraband" was being transported illegally and her family's business was suspected of facilitating this. However, the inspector told her that no trace of "contraband" had been found in any of the company premises which is why her apartments had become suspect. She was angry when they implied that her father was some sort of criminal. She could believe it of her brother: but to suspect her lovely father ... she found herself shouting expletives at the inspector for daring to make such a suggestion! They all cleared off after saying that her art store contained "nothing of interest".

She enjoyed the title of honorary President of the local art gallery but never bothered attending meetings to discuss the minutiae of their small company business. She had suggested to their chief curator that they might want to display some of her best paintings but accepted that he believed her creative imagination was too advanced for contemporary viewers. What surprised her, however, was when she noticed that the gallery's name had been changed. It had escaped her attention until one of her party friends remarked on the deletion of their family name which had occurred a few months after the visit by the police. She called to find out why but only received a vague explanation to do with reputational damage within the art world that she did not understand. There was nothing she could do about it and discovered, at the end of the year, that she was no longer listed as the gallery's honorary President.

She decided to attend a concert. She had read that the performers were meant to be very good although she knew nothing about them. She had read that the orchestra was one of the best in the world and the conductor was famous (she thought she may have heard his name ... perhaps on television?). She did not find the violin concerto easy listening and the program stated that the composer, Bartok, of whom she had never heard, had died in 1945. But the real distraction was Sajid who happened to be sitting directly in front of her. After the music had finished, Sajid turned and spoke to her. He behaved with that impeccable courtesy and grace that had first attracted her.

He asked if she had enjoyed the concert and she remembered that Sajid was, himself, a violinist. So, in reply, she asked how he would have interpreted the concerto if he had been the soloist. Sajid smiled and said with what she believed was an attractive humility that he could not have played the Bartok work as it was technically far too difficult for him. She assumed that he could have played it but just did not want to show off. She suggested that they went for a drink to catch up with what each other had been doing. Sajid, she learnt, had become a housing officer for the local council. One of his jobs was to investigate buildings that needed repair. She asked if he could look at the Tower because she thought it was beginning to show its age.

Sajid seemed reluctant to make any official investigation. He explained that his job was mainly looking at housing for homeless families, refugees, and asylum seekers. But, with pressure from his former girlfriend, he agreed to quietly make an informal assessment for her. She showed him how slow one of the eight elevators had become and how rubbish had accumulated outside some of the apartments down on the fortieth floor. Standing outside the offending apartments, Sajid was confronted by the residents who assumed that he was making an official check. They demanded that he tell the refuse collecting department to do their job and collect the rubbish they had been told to put outside their doors. Before he could explain that this was not his role, they were joined by residents from other floors who had witnessed Sajid's arrival. Soon, heated exchanges were taking place between floors forty-one and forty, joined within a few minutes by people from floors thirty to thirty-nine.

The television coverage of the fighting that overtook the Tower made it look worse than it was. No one was killed in the first two weeks, but those on the very top floors were uncomfortably aware of the disputes that had quickly consumed the attention of all the residents from floor twenty-five to fifty.

"What happens if there's a fire? We wouldn't be safe up here."

Although the window bars were intended to make accidental falls impossible, the police were called in the third week when Winnie White was defenestrated. A longshot photo of 'Winnie's window' was on the local newspaper's front page. Sajid asked his newly rediscovered girlfriend if Winnie White had anything to do with the drugs trade that was thought to be behind the 'storey wars'.

"Drugs?!" she exclaimed. "Surely there's no drugs problem at the Towers?! Do you think that's why they wanted to search my arts store?" she asked him.

Sajid said there were almost certainly going to be drug users amongst the huge numbers of residents in the Towers.

"Impossible!" she shouted. "People in my building are rich and famous. None of them could possibly be involved in crime."

After this outburst, she noticed that Sajid stopped visiting her. She told herself he was probably having to concentrate on perfecting his violin technique so that he could play what she had heard – Bartok was it? Anyway, this gave her more time to focus upon the creation of more artistic masterpieces that she lovingly locked away in her art store, alongside some "painting materials" her father had sent and asked her to look after.

"Tell no one about those expensive materials, let's make them a secret just between us" her dad said.

After dispatching her latest daringly experimental piece of acrylic upon tarmac, she sat back and frowned as she looked out across the city. Behind her, the chandelier rocked slowly from side to side and the paintings in the room adopted their familiarly skewed hanging. Everything felt different yet nothing had changed.

31

A TAIL TO TELL

At just over three meters in height, Jack's wife was a lot taller than him. However, Zaro was often heard complaining that she wished she were still taller to match the size of other Koplian women. To compensate for her feelings of inadequacy, she spent a great deal of time and money on the grooming of her tail.

Although both his parents came from Earth, Jack had been born and raised on Koplia: so, he was fully accustomed to the Koplian women's obsession with their tails. Some were long and thin and distinctly unattractive to the small community of Koplian men who lived apart in the faraway hillsides. Others were short and stubby, attracting the attention of those men who knew that they would never marry anyone else. But Zaro's was fat and long; so, she was able to select her partner and chose Jack as one of the exotic species who had come from a couple who had arrived from Earth a generation before. However, once married to the man she wanted, she started to talk ceaselessly about the problems of a Koplian woman who was shorter than average. "You must feel that you are married to a dwarf," she told Jack on more than one occasion.

Jack had learnt that the best way to diffuse the conversation about height was to compliment Zaro's tail. "There must be hundreds of women who would die to have a tail like yours," he would counter. And Zaro would draw herself up to her full height, curl her tail round her body, and smile. "Perhaps I should have it smoothed at the beautician tomorrow," she would say; and Jack would nod in approval.

There were scores of beauticians in the Koplian capital. Zaro had been to most of them and frequently moaned that none of them could give her the satisfaction that she sought. Of course, they could smooth her tail, but she felt she was seeking more from them. On returning home, she told Jack that she would try another place next week because this last one was just not good enough. Jack appeared to pay attention as she listed all the things that Zaro, now an expert on beauty techniques, said was wrong with this last establishment. But he already knew what his wife would say, so perhaps was not paying all the attention that he could. Which is why he automatically nodded in agreement when she said it might be a good idea to try an out-of-town beautician.

Like the women of the capital, those who lived nearer the hills wore no clothes. Koplia's climate was so hot, and tails were so prominent, that clothing would always have been an impediment. Jack's parents, like other Earthlings, had continued the practice of wearing clothes and Jack – brought up by these caring people – kept a small supply of garments to wear when he left the house. Zaro found this practice amusing, even slightly titillating. She even regarded her husband's vain attempts to persuade her to stop going out naked something of an affront to her inherited culture. However, more from a wicked wish to attract his attention (she did not believe he was really listening the last time she spoke to him) she covered her chest and back with a giant piece of cloth as she left for the beautician. "I'm just off now," she called to Jack who was reading the newspaper and had not looked up. "See you soon," he called back without seeing her daring experiment into fashion.

Zaro was annoyed. Jack had not even noticed her attempt to make a joke out of his obsession with getting dressed. She stomped her way down the street, attracting derisory comments from neighbors who had never seen a Koplian woman with a shawl. Hearing their jibes, she defiantly continued to wear it, lashing her tail around in a gesture that said; "if you dare insult me to my face, you'll receive a crack around the head with this long, fat weapon!" No one challenged her openly and she made her way to the transit station to catch a hovership out of town. As the craft lifted off, Zaro could see the twin suns rising above the towers of the city. Then with a dipping of its wings, the hovership turned and sped away towards the hills.

Jack finished reading his paper, washed a few dishes from breakfast, and made his way down the street towards the coffee bar that his parents and other ex-patriots had established on their new planet. Unlike Koplian men who brought up the children and worked as beauticians, Earthling males had continued the hot climate tradition of spending most of their time sipping strong coffee whilst lazing away their time in idle chatter. Jack sat happily with a few of his mates for the rest of the morning discussing why his team had lost last night's match against their arch-rivals and disagreeing with others who asserted that it was because the rivals played better. He preferred to blame the decisions of the referee whom he accused of bias, being bribed, and having the eyes of a blind salamander (the sort that frequented Koplian caves and never saw the light of day). It was not until the afternoon that his attention was suddenly arrested by the images projected onto the café vidscreen.

Zaro had never visited an out-of-town beautician. In fact, out-of-town beauticians, who were almost all hillside cavemen, rarely if ever saw a Koplian woman from the capital. Certainly, the one whom Zaro decided to try had never seen a tail like Zaro's. His own wife had a short, stubby one and both his daughters had decidedly stunted varieties that had no chance of growing to the luxuriant length and breadth of Zaro's. He welcomed her into his establishment and pushed her to the front of the queue that had begun to form outside. He knew that his prestige would be greatly enhanced if others could see him catering for a tail this large and plentiful.

The one aspect that puzzled him was the covering that Zaro was wearing over her shoulders and breasts. Perhaps this was a novelty that women from the capital had introduced that had not yet reached the provinces. He had never operated on a woman who was wrapped in cloth. He supposed that he was expected to remove it gently before getting to work. Zaro, on the other hand, had quite forgotten that she was wearing the shawl. Inside she was still fuming about Jack's apparent indifference to her concerns regarding height. As the beautician touched her shoulders to remove the garment, she became aware that this little man was able to reach that high – a reminder that if she were another half meter taller, he would never have managed it.

Her response was automatic – she had no intention of harming him but clipped him with the tip of her tail. The power of the tail threw him across the room, crashing through the glass window. He landed shaken but unhurt on the pavement where a small, peering crowd of onlookers had gathered to admire Zaro's tail. Zaro got up to apologize; but it was too late. The crowd outside had already decided that she had assaulted one of their friends. She was a foreigner from the city: now she was seen as an arrogant harlot who wore strange clothes and had deliberately hurt a respected member of their community.

With their stubby tails flashing before them, the local women walked towards Zaro. She was cornered in the beautician's parlor and startled by the vengeful looks from the threatening group. She scanned the room for a way out or some way of defending herself. She began by pushing the chairs across the room to form a temporary barrier between her and her assailants. She hoped that this would give time for them to hear her protests of innocence. But they ignored her words. All that they saw was a woman of their height who was showing off a tail of which any of them would be proud. The beautician, now fully recovered, shouted that he was unharmed, and they should leave his shop so that he could attend his customer. But none of them paid any attention to this little man. It was Zaro who was responsible for upsetting their community, it was her fault that they were stuck out here in the sticks with small tails and pathetic, cavemen husbands. She was going to pay for all their troubles.

When the robot police arrived, they found several local women heaped up on the ground outside the beautician and a bloody but unbowed woman from the capital flailing a strip of cloth like a bullfighter, daring anyone else to come and fight her. The stubby tails had made some impact on her, but her giant weapon had had a terrifying effect when used in the enclosed space of the parlor. Only one or two assailants could reach her at a time, so she had dealt with them by tossing them through the same window through which she had inadvertently pushed the shop owner. She knew better than to fight with the robots who politely asked her to accompany them to the police station. Their stun guns were at the ready for any resistance, so she walked with them down the street whilst onlookers and vidnews robots clustered around to see what all the fuss was about. It was this news footage that caught Jack's attention as he put down his coffee cup.

Jack was rarely riled by his compatriots. He was known as an easygoing fellow who had never shown any desire to fly back to his parental home planet. He was seen as a contented husband who might one day become a happy father and raise interestingly cross-bred Koplian/Earthling children.

Meanwhile, his conversation over coffee was reasonably entertaining and always inoffensive. So, his sudden extremely rude exclamation of surprise when he saw the vidscreen showing his injured wife being led off to a police station caught everyone's attention.

"Where are they taking her?" he cried. His mates shook their heads in disbelief.

"You can't let these robots drag your wife away," they replied.

The news showed Zaro near the hills. "They've taken her out of the city!" the café owner shouted.

Jack was astonished. Why had the police taken her out of the capital? Maybe she had been kidnapped by the cave people and their local robots in a show of strength against the female rulers in the city. There had been rumors of unrest circulating for some time and had been reported in his newspaper. Jack jumped to a conclusion and announced that he intended to get his wife back ... would anyone care to help him? Soon he and his cronies had formed an unlikely band of vigilantes. Setting off towards the hovership station, they marched along with a determination that amused the passing Koplian women towering above them.

In the hovership, the men discussed tactics. Should they come to the police station *en masse* and surprise the sedentary robot guards? Should they make a formal request for Zaro's release before making any show of strength? Should they assess the strength of local opposition before making any move? Should they consider that their lack of tail – let alone stun guns – might make them a rather feeble platoon against powerful forces ranged against them in the unfamiliar territory of the hill?

By the time the hovership came to a standstill, their determination to force the issue had cooled and they left the craft with some trepidation. Their fears were more than justified when the women whom Zaro had dumped onto the street spied this group of diminutive earthmen who had suddenly appeared from nowhere. They surrounded them and demanded to know what they wanted. Jack, looked up at their leader and said – in a quiet but defiant voice – that he had come to see why his wife had been arrested. The robot police returned a few minutes later to find a few injured Earthmen lying in the street with local Koplian women jubilantly parading the captured husband of the formidable Zaro between them.

There are many accounts of what happened next. Some say that Jack was and always had been an expert in electronics and was able to disable the robots in a demonstration of subversive power that could threaten the very foundations of Koplian society – a notion that I believe should be discounted. Some say that the robot police who had been out to deal with the two disturbances had not been serviced for some time and failed to function properly. Others believe that the women, drunk with their recent victory, turned on the robot police who had come to arrest them. Whatever the reason, when Jack was deposited in front of the leading robot's tracks in a show of bravado by the women, the robot stopped and attempted to pick Jack up. It failed. And this was the moment that the vidscreen news showed the robot tipping over amongst the mêlée of women and, after a brief spark of distress, dying on the street. The women backed away instinctively, awaiting the stun guns of the following robots to open up. But instead, they all followed their leader's example, tipped over, and lay still. The women fled before police reinforcements could arrive. But none appeared. Jack picked himself up and, with his walking wounded colleagues, made his way to the now deserted police station. He unlocked a cell door and released the sole prisoner, his wife. The vidnews carried pictures of the proud band, escorting a puzzled Zaro, marching back to the hovership station.

Koplian politics had always been a puzzle to Earth observers. When the two planets first made contact, it was clear that however complex Earth government had been in the past, it rarely reached the Byzantine and labyrinthine depths of their newfound friends in the galaxy. Whatever the issue, there were always disputes that found supporters moving from one group to another depending on totally different concerns. And so it was when Jack's band was seen marching in triumph towards the hovership station. Even before they arrived back in the city, there were already fierce debates taking place about how an Earthman had managed to destroy an entire station of robot police and force a fierce group of local women to flee. Suggestions were made that he and his followers had developed as yet undetected weapons of considerable force. Zaro was depicted by some as a covert supporter of a new movement that intended to undermine Koplian society – and even lead an invasion from the planet that they said was Jack's real home, Earth.

By the time that Zaro was back home with her heroic husband, the Radical Hillside Cave party had formed an unlikely alliance with the Imperial Galactic party to demand immediate action from the weakened government of Tailed Feminists who had ruled from the capital with the disintegrating support of the Beauticians Union for many years. Before the night was out, the government had fallen, and the new alliance had taken control. Ignoring protests from the small ex-patriot Earth community, they demanded that Earth provide proof that they were not behind the attack on the hillside community that had been led by the agent provocateur, Jack. Unable to disprove a negative, Earth politicians sought desperately to disassociate themselves from anything that they were told had happened at the hillside community the day before. Koplian battle cruisers were dispatched and surrounded Earth as Zaro and Jack were eating breakfast. Unaware of the situation, Zaro decided to take the day off work whilst she recuperated from the extraordinary struggles she had endured the day before. So, Jack walked to the café to see if his compatriots had recovered, and they could bask in the glory of their recent adventure. He arrived just in time to watch the live coverage of stubby-tailed cruiser pilots launching their bulldoze weapons that disintegrated his parent's planet within two minutes.

My job, as official historian of Earthlings and other non-Koplian life forms has been greatly hampered by the destruction of all record of Earth's history and cultures. However, I have managed to piece together a little from the accounts given by the small ex-patriot community here, many of whom we now have safely locked up in jail. I can assert it is already clear that the Earthling disdain for tailed creatures has been adequately punished by the quick action of our brave pilots. The new alliance government prevented the invasion by Earthlings which would have inevitably followed once they believed that Jack and his friends had developed a weapon of mass destruction capable of defeating Koplian security forces. So now we are safe again to enjoy the fruits of our civilization, the skills of our beauticians and the admiration of our little men.

32

ETIQUETTE

"Phipps!" Johnson called. "Who is that incredibly attractive woman with the royal party?" Johnson had seen her first out of the corner of his eye when being introduced to the King's press attaché. It was the sort of glimpse that makes you want to turn around to check that your vision is in order. He had resisted just long enough to shake hands with the official but, upon turning, she was gone.

"She is the Princess Sunev, sir." Phipps had known the journalist for years as he always stayed at the Imperial when being sent to cover stories in the region. Phipps always made a point of letting all journalists know that he was a potent source of information tips became his most lucrative form of income when they were in town. And plenty of them had come to cover the royal visit.

Johnson felt a breath of anxiety on hearing how exalted was her birth. The royals were exotically dressed and performed complicated and lengthy daily rituals upon meeting foreigners. But Sunev stood out in his eyes when, eventually, he had managed to gaze at her in full view. She walked slowly with her hips always thrust forward. Her long, black hair accentuated her powerfully browed forehead. Green eyes set in a soft brown face with high cheekbones ... a flowing, multi-colored gown ... an impression of strength and aggression contrasting strangely with delicately tapered wrists and ankles. Overcoming his feeling of inferiority, he asked Phipps how he might get to meet her.

"An introduction could be arranged," Phipps informed him and Johnson put the down-payment on what was to be the sort of tip that only people like Phipps ever receive. "However, I feel I should make you aware of her reputation, sir. She has been brought up to uphold the thousand-year-old traditions of her people. She practices all the rituals to ensure that foreigners do not erode their way of life. You may be disappointed if you expect anything other than the most formal reception. Her reputation is one of always having her own way."

Johnson said that he understood but, in fact, he felt challenged. He was, after all, an international journalist with a formidable reputation of his own. The only person he had ever been afraid of was the wizened owner-editor of the paper for which he worked. And the editor had sent him to interview characters like Sunev. "Why not combine work with pleasure?" he thought to himself.

The next day, Phipps had somehow arranged a private audience for Johnson. As Sunev went through the exaggerated movements of the purification ceremony, Johnson felt increasingly aroused by what he perceived as a grave but erotic dance. Speech between them had to be conducted through an interpreter a person of indeterminate age and gender clothed entirely in black and talking in a piping monotone. Despite this drawback, Johnson did manage to convey to Sunev that his interest in her was not just as a professional journalist. She explained in a poised and polite tone, that in her country there were three acceptable expressions of male interest in a woman of her standing. In order of increasing seriousness, they were:

- I would bow down for you
- I would lie before you and do your command.
- I would die to be consumed by your passion.

The interpreter chirped in: "The Princess Sunev would advise that you restrain your expressions of adoration to the level of bowing." He got up, and in a measured way, bowed lowly to the wonderful woman. For the first time, she smiled broadly showing her perfect teeth glinting in the noon-day light. He requested a further audience, and this was granted.

He told Phipps about the audience and his plans for the next assignation. Phipps asked if all this was going to be reported in his newspaper. "Well, I suppose that depends on where it all leads," smirked Johnson, and he walked off leaving Phipps shaking his head with undisguised disapproval. At the end of the second audience, Johnson melodramatically flung himself full-length upon the floor, calling out that he would carry out her command. Sunev did not smile but sat, completely immobile, except for a slight extension of her ringed middle finger towards the interpreter. The interpreter rose as Johnson asked if he could see Sunev again. The little piping voice informed him that if he would do her command, then there would be no more arranged meetings. He would simply have to come the moment she called. With these words, the androgynous companion left, and the Princess sat, motionless, waiting for him to leave. He scrambled to his feet and departed backwards.

Two days passed. Johnson's editor was becoming irritable. He left messages for his employee to hurry up with the article. But he heard nothing. Johnson was spending his time avoiding the dreaded employer's messages whilst ensuring that he would always be around if and when Sunev called. Phipps was well aware of the journalist's dilemma and made sure that all communications to Johnson were channeled through him. Eventually he knocked at the sleepless man's door.

"Your editor has sent an express telegram ordering you to contact him immediately and the Princess Sunev commands your instant presence."

Johnson sprang up. "I'm going to her now," he cried. "Phipps, phone my editor and say anything to stop him harassing me!"

That evening Phipps phoned the editor. "I have to inform you, sir, that Mr. Johnson will not be writing his story. His infatuation with the Princess Sunev led him to propose marriage to her two days ago. Fortunately, however, she put him out of his misery. Tonight, when he declared that he would die for her, she ate him."

33

GRENDON

The Grendon was the strangest creature Joseph had ever come across. Extraterrestrial beings often visited the planet but usually kept their distance. Joseph was well-known for having claimed contact with many of them. But most regarded him as an eccentric dreamer and took little notice of his occasional claims.

"Honestly, I've met many of them," he told the local tv journalist sent to do an amusing feature on a man about whom viewers could have a little giggle at the end of the local news.

But the Grendon appeared one night in a flurry of wind and sand. Joseph was not perturbed by the stranger's arrival. None had ever harmed him, and some had spoken in his own language with scarcely a hint of foreign accent.

"Why do you want to speak to me?" he asked.

The Grendon did not speak. It communicated in a way that he had never experienced. It was as if it was talking from inside his own head.

"I have been watching you. You are a creature that other humans seem to regard with suspicion. Why do they believe that you are plotting against others? Do you know why that is the case?"

Joseph had to think about this question. At first, he wondered if the Grendon was referring to the article lampooning his claims of meeting non-terrestrial beings. But mention of plotting reminded him of strange people who seemed to think he was within a vast network of conspirators wanting to take control of the planet.

"You must mean the idiots who believe that there is a secret society that plans to seize power. I have no idea why people hold these irrational beliefs. I assume it is because these are ideas fed to them by genuinely powerful people who want to deflect attention from their own positions of power."

The Grendon seemed to swirl upwards like a tiny tornado before settling back like a cloud on the ground. The Grendon appeared to grumble before asking: "What would you do if you had the power that these conspiracy theorists believe you have?"

Joseph scratched his head. When he was much younger, he had studied history in a famous University that introduced him to an infamous tract entitled 'The Protocols of the Elders of Zion." He remembered how it had been used to build upon centuries of anti-Semitism to reinforce the idea that

Jews like him somehow met in secret to take control of the World. He spoke disdainfully to the Grendon.

"People who believe they can somehow make the word better by seizing power always seem to end up as worse than those they are determined to replace."

The Grendon seemed to laugh – it was a horrible gurgle that rose up from inside him. It made him feel slightly nauseous. The Grendon recognized this instantly and apologized. "Sorry about that. I dd not mean to make you feel ill. I simply wondered whether you have much to lose."

"What do you mean?"

"I think you have a saying "one may as well hang for a sheep as a lamb". You already have all the disadvantages of being distrusted as a secret plotter but without any of the advantages of controlling through this non-existent conspiracy. So, how would you feel if you were granted these powers?

Joseph smirked. "Then all the suspicions of the idiotic conspiracy theorists would be proved correct!"

The Grendon seemed to roll around on the ground. Joseph frowned as he watched this display.

"Grendon, are you laughing?"

"I was enjoying the irony. But I still want to know your answer."

Joseph scratched his head. "What on earth would you do? Are you saying you could accomplish deeds impossible for we humans?"

"Not really. A Grendon can destroy but not construct. If you want anything positive, you'll have to do that yourself.

But I can dispose of all those conspiracy theorists and evil men who hold power in your nations."

"You mean you can kill people at my bidding?"

"Yes"

"But that would leave me no better than the awful men you would be murdering."

"Well, it would not really seem like murder. Everyone would think it was natural causes, or old age, or an unfortunate infection. No one would suspect you."

Joseph thought about this. He certainly felt tempted. The list of dictators inflicting pain and death upon thousands of people did not strike him as men who deserved to survive. If this Grendon could quietly dispose of these disgusting examples of humanity, Joseph could not see that anything worse would be the result. On the other hand, the people who put these creatures in charge of their countries would probably simply replace one devil with another. And Joseph himself would have done nothing other than confirm the worst suspicions of the crazy conspiracy theorists.

The Grendon read all Joseph's thoughts. Rising slowly into the sky, the Grendon left Joseph with a parting thought. "Very well, you are a good and thoughtful man. I shall leave you now and will not return."

The Grendon seemed to dissipate like a cloud of smoke. Joseph breathed a sigh of relief. He did not enjoy the dilemmas presented by beings like the Grendon. He never knew what the right answer was.

The next day, the newspapers were full of the unexpected news of the death of the leaders of two of the most powerful nations. The following days saw similar news from major nations. Some thought it was the result of a new pandemic that only seemed to affect older, over-powerful males. Some attributed it to a shadowy secret society with invisible tentacles that reached into the darkest reaches of the best protected citadels guarding men against all-comers day and night. Joseph decided that he would keep his conscience clean by telling about the Grendon in a short story that, despite being read by millions, was written off as the fantasy of an elderly science fiction writer.

34

HEADS

She had the most perfect body Mark had ever seen. Her delicately tapered shoulders seemed to flow into the curve of her back. And her long legs swelled and blossomed as they reached her shapely wheels. Her soft, musical voice spoke about those things which they both held dear their love, their allotment and food. "I am passionate about your peanut, parsley and pepper pasta, my love." The great klaxon voice that belonged to her second mouth she used to call him when he was working a few miles away in the orchards. Although Mark was only a human chef, he had summoned up the courage to ask this Zargon Princess to marry him. Her happy acceptance of his offer had brought his life undreamt-of fulfilment.

Mark's work colleagues were envious of his marriage to Princess Shula. Like most humans, they tried to associate with Zargons and copied their ways if they could. And the

Zargons had always been pleased to befriend the clumsy Earthlings whom they had discovered only a century before. Initial human fear and hostility to the aliens had slowly been replaced by the acceptance of Zargon superiority in virtually everything that Earth civilizations held most dear.

Technological comparisons were pointless. Zargon science was as far from 22nd century Earth knowledge as ours was from medieval alchemists. Our educational and cultural complexities, of which we are so proud, they appeared to assimilate with humor and understanding. Their enjoyment of our languages, our music and our religions was like that of an adult rediscovering half-forgotten but much-loved pieces of childhood in a cozy attic.

After a generation of living amongst us, their appearance no longer upset anyone. Now, of course, the Zargon body is regarded as the yardstick by which beauty is measured. When they heard the old adage "Two heads are better than one", they poked gentle fun at those who described their arrival as some sort of diabolical invasion. Their broad shoulders carry their twin heads with dignity and grace. Each head can turn round 360° degrees, and they frequently roll along looking in two directions at once. Each head needs some time to sleep and dream; but both heads are rarely unconscious at the same time. When asked about the extraordinary gap between human and Zargon knowledge, they smile and say that they have twice as much thinking time as those on Earth.

Shula is slightly smaller than most Zargons nearly two meters tall on her bare wheels. But she can speed along with the fastest with her powerfully tracked mercedes (I am unsure why this name was given to Zargon wheels a hundred years ago). Zargons have always been anxious not to offend humans and try not to refer to what they see as the peculiarities of our bodies. But even they find it hard to hide their curiosity about our feet. When Mark wakes up, he often finds Shula counting his toes. "They are like little pink artichokes: shall I lick them?" Often, she strokes them and asks if he can feel anything. Because their physiology precludes it, Zargons do not seem to understand tickling.

Amongst Zargons, it is no secret why Shula married Mark. But to humans, her decision is almost incomprehensible. To most of us, Mark is a quiet unassuming cook who grows his own fruit and vegetables. He works in the hotel and is regarded as an excellent head chef. But he does not aspire to all those things which we praise most highly. He is only average height and not remarkably strong. His academic abilities are not outstanding, and his family are not endowed with great wealth. When asked, none of his former girlfriends told the local newspaper that Mark had been their sexiest partner; although the national papers offered to pay considerable sums for interesting intimate details when it became known that he was marrying a Zargon princess. His prowess as a fighter was revealed when a drunken customer used foul language about Shula in the hotel. Mark demanded that the man be quiet. Mark's black eye and cut lip were quickly repaired whilst his pride was not.

Shula tended her wounded hero. "Why did you fight?" she asked.

"The man insulted you," Mark said as if this were an explanation.

"So, the cuts and bruises you have suffered in some way balance the insults I have suffered?"

"No, Shula. But you can't let men like that get away with saying such things unchallenged."

"Why is that, Mark? Are you saying that the people in the hotel would believe these terrible things about me unless you let the man punch your face?"

"I didn't say that. Of course, nobody thinks badly of you at work. But I could not stand to think of your being hurt."

Shula laughed. And Mark felt a little foolish. The thought of the drunk attempting to harm Shula brought back the century-old image of armed men regressing into gun-toting rapists as they attacked the first Zargon women to land on Earth. These warriors had never spoken of the depth of their humiliation at the hands of the Zargon women: but their meek return to human society had destroyed the Earth's age-old macho culture.

"I am more worried about you getting hurt," Shula said as she stroked Mark's lip. "After all, you are the celebrity."

When Zargons visit Earth, they usually go to Mark and Shula's house. People assume that this is to pay their respects to the Princess and Zargons are happy for us to believe this. But Shula knows that it is to meet her famous husband. Mark's reputation is one of near genius: but not on Earth. It is on Zargon where Mark's true worth is appreciated. Not everyone understands how important food is to Zargons. Their culture has evolved to incorporate everything that Earth can offer but Zargon taste buds are so much more sensitive than humans that culinary brilliance is valued above everything else.

"I would do anything for a taste of your coriander and carrot soup, my love."

There is a story about a Zargon ambassador who cut short his discussions about intergalactic transport and defense with the United Nations President to spend a day with Shula and Mark. He implied that it was his duty to honor the Princess. But as he departed, he was overheard to have said, "Cucumber and courgettes couscous with cream: wait till I tell them at home!"

As a young man, Mark had been taken to Zargon along with hundreds of other trainee chefs to complete their education. The end-of-course assessment required the production of an original dish to be tasted by a Zargon panel. Not surprisingly, only Zargon trainees ever got to the final stages of the competition to award the culinary master-chef prize. The finals were watched and tasted all over the planet through tactovision and Mark's were the first dishes prepared by a human to reach this stage. There was intense excitement as the panel of Zargon super-tasters experimented with the texture, feel and stimulation factors of all the meals prepared by the finalists. Princess Shula was not only the royal presenter of the prize; she was also one of the most gifted of the super-tasters. She told Mark some years later that the first time she had held his vegetable surprise in one of her mouths, it had been the most erotic experience of her life. His elevation to the ranks of the Zargon élite accompanied his winning first prize. But it was the interview conducted afterwards that made his name a legend in Zargon culture.

It was customary for the interviewer to ask great chefs about their secret ingredients. Zargon cooks always became wonderfully evasive with this question, hence retaining a degree of mystery around their art. When asked, Mark gave the bluntest and most memorable reply about his vegetable surprise that won not only Shula's heart, but also the affection of the entire community. He held up a pair of cauliflowers – a familiar Zargon vegetable. And he said: "When making vegetable surprise with cauliflower, two heads are better than one."

35

JUAREZ

To criticize Juarez's art as obsessive seems as absurd as criticizing the sky for being blue. Juarez came to painting quite late in life and his one great subject fills his canvases and overwhelms the viewer when his work is seen *en masse* in a gallery. The critic who penned the article in the local Rio newspaper and attacked Juarez for his "obsession" has long since been forgotten. However, I doubt if Juarez will be forgotten so soon.

Juarez has described how his adult life had been totally normal. Every day, he and his wife rose at five o'clock, washed quickly and ate a frugal breakfast. Then at six, he walked down the sandy track from his two-roomed house to catch the bus on the main highway whilst his wife climbed the hill to the church. He went to work whilst she prayed for a child. He stood in the packed bus as it lurched its way to the city center to arrive soon after eight. He stopped for a coffee at the same bar every day, then walked around the corner to start work at half past eight: or nine o'clock if the bus were delayed.

Always good with figures, Juarez was placed in the accounts department. He had few friends at work. By the time he began painting, he was about twenty years older than anyone there. Their conversation was primarily about football (which he disliked) and their conquest of women other than their wives (which he found distasteful). He consumed his lunch alone at the local coffee bar and caught the bus for home at five o'clock. His wife prepared their dinner for nine: they watched television for an hour before retiring for bed. Nothing in his life prepared him for what happened next.

He described to me how he had begun dreaming of a young woman. It was not his wife. He had dared not speak about this recurring dream as he knew it would upset her. But the dreams did not fade. Instead, they became more intense every night. He dreamt that she was walking before him and pointing to objects too distant for him to see. Another time, she and he linked arms. She smiled at him and asked him if he liked her dress. She always appeared wearing the same dress with its distinctive blue pattern on a clean, white background. One lunchtime, instead of walking to the coffee bar, Juarez began doodling on a sheet of paper. He was trying to draw the face of the unknown woman. After several attempts, he gave up as his technique was so poor. But he felt better for having tried to capture his vision.

Still childless, his wife told him that a new priest was coming to the church and that she hoped that his intercession might alter their luck. Juarez improvised an excuse for taking up drawing at home. He said that he wanted to try to picture how their daughter might look. So, putting her image on paper might also help to bring about her birth. His wife accepted this explanation for his new hobby and took an interest in the appearance of the girl whom she wished to see running about their house. Juarez's talent for precise and intricate drawing soon became apparent. Despite these being interpretations of dreams, the imagery took on a clarity that became the hallmark of his later paintings.

Juarez began buying paints and canvases only after he had visited an art gallery during his lunch break. He had taken it into his head that the dream woman might be a well-known character and that he had simply internalized the image one day without realizing it. Perhaps another artist had already painted her, and the canvas was on display. If he walked into the gallery and saw her as she had originally been painted, then maybe his dreams would leave him, and he could return to his former, untroubled existence. But she was not on the walls of the gallery. Instead, for the first time he saw what color could bring to an image if the artist used oil paints. He determined to do the same in the hope that this would at last exorcise the woman from his mind.

The flood of paintings that followed filled their house. Neighbors asked if they could hang them on their walls and his wife gladly let them unclutter her rooms. Perhaps the profusion of images, like icons of prayer, would at last bring a daughter to them. But no daughter arrived, and the dreams never ceased. It was one of his larger canvases that was brought to my attention. As curator of one of the galleries designed by our greatest architect, Oscar Niemeyer, I was always on the lookout for new Brazilian talent. One of Juarez's neighbors had decided that she might be able to make a little money if she sold the painting that had been loaned to her. It showed the dream woman floating above the Rio skyline. Slightly Chagall-like in its imagery, it was unlike Marc Chagall in that every detail was drawn with the exactitude of a dedicated accountant. The dealer who bought it was a friend of mine. When he showed it to me, I immediately determined to try to find the artist.

Juarez was not hard to trace. The seller of the painting had left details of where she lived. Like an amateur detective, I drove out to the far-off neighborhood in search of the elusive painter. I thought it might take days to find him. Instead, almost everyone in the area knew exactly where he and his wife lived; and were able to show me examples of his work that bedecked their walls. When I introduced myself to Juarez that evening, I was welcomed in by the wife as if I were the harbinger of good news and the bringer of good fortune. Juarez just looked tired after his long day and asked what interest I could have in his paintings. I described my job and suggested that we might like to work together to create a small exhibition of his paintings. His wife became very excited and encouraged her husband to accept. Juarez seemed more hesitant: but he came round to the idea when I was inspired to throw up a novel idea. I suggested that the woman's image shown on the walls of a great gallery might help him find more peace than he seemed to enjoy at present. With hindsight I can see that I could not have been more mistaken.

The exhibition was a sensation. International interest was generated by a photographic montage of his work being shown on television abroad. With people coming from Europe and the USA to see this new artist, local people who rarely if ever visited the gallery came flocking in to see what all the fuss was about. Juarez continued to work in the accounts department until his fame spread to his work colleagues. They teased him about the sexual exploits they imagined he had achieved with the now famous young woman whose face had appeared in magazines and newspapers. He quit the job as he found that his income from the sale of paintings more than made up for the loss of salary.

We became friends. I would talk with him about the art world, and he would occasionally describe to me how it felt to be haunted every night by the same unknown woman. I asked him if he thought she was, as his wife suggested, the image of the daughter who had never arrived. He shook his head and admitted that he had always known that this was not true. I suggested that he might have seen her when he was a child and the image had re-emerged from his far-off memory. He shrugged his shoulders and said he could not know but, despite many attempts, he could not recall anyone quite like her. "Why do you think she is always wearing the same dress?" My query was spurred by the appearance of the same styled dress in Rio shops. Juarez said that he liked the pattern but had no idea where it had come from.

The 'Juarez dress', as it came to be known, earned the artist no money at all. Despite his having created the pattern in his paintings, there was nothing to prevent the unscrupulous fashion business exploiting his work. So, for some years Juarez was tormented by seeing young women whom he thought might be his dream come to life. He would rush up to them, only to find that their face revealed someone quite different. His wife had at last given up all hope of conceiving a child and was becoming concerned at her husband's embarrassing behavior. His continual pestering of strange women suggested to her that as an ageing male, he felt he needed the company of young women to make him believe he was still young. But she was wrong. He desired only to find one woman – then he could sleep without her ceaseless walking through his dreams.

The dream became a nightmare in the way that only we, in Brazil, know how. The precision with which Juarez illustrated the woman's face suggested a deeper knowledge of her life than if he had actually known her in the flesh. The exact curve of the cheek, the delicacy of her lips and nose, the open-eyed clarity of her brow – all these were shown in such detail that plastic surgeons could bring about near-perfect copies at a very reasonable price. The number of women paying to make their face look like Juarez's dream is thought to have totaled over a thousand. Most of them sported Juarez dresses leaving the artist in dread of walking the streets of Rio.

"Nothing is worse than having your dreams become reality," he said. "I shall never know if I have met the woman now. Even if she walked up to me and described our dream life together, I would not know if she were just some facsimile who had studied all my paintings."

He and his wife had moved out of their poor dwelling and now lived in an apartment in the fashionable neighborhood of Urca. His paintings had earned him enough to retire and live comfortably and afforded his wife a little compensation for having remained childless. Urca housed older residents who tended to resist the craze in Juarez dresses and plastic surgery. So, he could walk the local streets in the day without seeing distorted reminders of his nights. But the death of his wife brought him to the point of madness. The loss of his life companion was bad enough; but the news of her passing inspired numerous dream simulations to travel into Urca to make intimate proposals to the famous artist. This is what nearly drove him over the edge.

I suppose that I felt some guilt as it was I who had first brought him from obscurity into the fierce glare of celebrity. So, I arranged for Juarez to take a long holiday. No one was told to where he had fled, so he was left untroubled for the year it took for him to regain his sanity. He lived in the house that my parents had left me in a quiet corner of Minas Gerais. Here he was able to paint and exist with the assistance of a local maid who knew nothing about art, nor of the man's fame. His final works show a more peaceful scene in which the woman appears happier with the world around her. He let me have a number of these wonderful works that now hang in my living room.

His return to Rio was heralded by the local newspaper as if he was again giving his blessing to the city he had abandoned. In fact, he missed the company of the sensible people of Urca and rarely ventured outside the locality into Rio's rushing streets. And suddenly he stopped painting. I thought his dream woman might have at long decided to leave him in peace. I asked him why he had decided to hang up his brushes and was saddened by the reply. "I can still see her every night," he told me. "But in the morning, I see very little as my eyes are failing me. I cannot see the canvases; the colors all seem indistinct. So, I must stop now. Perhaps she will let me go soon." And he smiled as if he might discover her true identity only after he had rejoined his wife.

36

THE OBSERVER

Evolution on the distant planet, Soggy, was driven by the constant daylight of its three suns. The protecting atmosphere was suffused with the rainwater charged up from the plentiful oceans. The vegetation that spread from the seas up onto the barren land developed its own characteristic means of reproduction: the production of vast clouds of spores. Over several million years, the spores had evolved by clumping together and generating a sophisticated, permanent presence in the air. This "brain" constantly replaced dead filaments with new spores that grew from the plantations that the clever vegetables had colonized on the hillsides.

Their friends, the walking trees, were less clever but helped when it came to establishing shaded areas for the young. At their age, the youngsters preferred to show off their petals rather than develop the disciplines required to join the floating spore collective. They could not appreciate the phenomenal innovations that their parents had achieved. Driven by sunlight and starlight, the spores had managed to send small spore clouds to fly at unimaginable speed through much of the galaxy before returning to report on what they had experienced. Whilst many planets seemed almost lifeless, reports from one called Earth seemed worth further investigation.

Although the spread of mammalian life forms seemed clumsy and ridiculously underdeveloped, the spores thought that exploring the planet could help them understand different ways of travelling than those they had created. None of the mammalian life forms seemed able to float through the air although bird flight looked like a cheap alternative. None of them seemed able to float through hyperspace although reports of huge firework displays leading to metal tubes being blown into space seemed an expensive and unnecessarily dangerous alternative.

Very carefully one night the spores placed a small bunch of youngsters in a position to observe what seemed like the most advanced creation of the primitive life forms. With their excited sepals straining to observe, the forward exploratory expedition made a close examination of the wheels of a bus that went round and round, round and round, round and round; the wheels of the bus went round and round all day long.

37

SACRED FLAME

Jan Jumbly was an official historian. There were only six official historians. Acquiring one of these top posts was the pinnacle of an academic career. Jan's pride in her work never interfered with her openness to criticism from any of the other five. They all knew that the only way of ensuring the integrity of their accounts was by continual, systematic evaluation of each other's work. In addition, an independent audit of the processes and procedures, both traditional and innovative, that each were free to introduce was put in place. As a result, depending upon the latest study, opinions regarding any aspect of history swung first one way, then the other.

Jan's special subject was the war. Apart from the never-ending debates carried on between the six of them, no one was any longer interested in how the war had begun. It had simply become a permanent feature of national life. Casualty lists appeared on the government website each week, and Jan cross-checked the life details of every individual before they were cremated in Sacred Flame.

The Enemy had no regard for Sacred Flame. They had no official historians, merely journalist hacks whose accounts were monitored by Jan. She illustrated how their simplistic stories were frequently untrue but still effective tools of propaganda against Sacred Flame.

Jan's study of casualty trends was analyzed and reviewed by fellow historians. She demonstrated how the introduction of robot soldiers whose Artificial Intelligence far outstripped any normal squaddie's capacity to decide upon effective courses of action during a battle had transformed Sacred Flame cremation sources. In the early days of the war, many years before Jan had been born, frontline soldiers headed casualty lists. Over the past decades, however, deaths were primarily caused amongst civilians caught up in skirmishes about which they knew nothing until it was too late for them to flee.

Jan's sister and esteemed colleague, Dawn, had made an intensive study of the development of Artificial Intelligence. Her thesis showed there was no difference between the level of sophistication achieved by enemy Artificial Intelligence compared to Sacred Flame. Therefore, stalemate was to be expected in the war as long as military Artificial Intelligence dominated the tactics and strategy of both sides. Jan's counter thesis suggested that Artificial Intelligence advances were staggered. This ensured that at any one moment, either Sacred Flame or Enemy would hold an advantage until the other side caught up and overtook in a never-ending game of leapfrog.

She argued that presence of casualties was proof of this game because permanent equality would result in zero casualties on both sides. Instead, equality only occurred for an instant every few weeks whilst the balance tipped one way, then the other.

Despite attempts to remain outside the focus of public scrutiny and gossip, both Jan and Dawn were easy targets for publicists on both sides. Jan was accused of being an Enemy infiltrator 'why else would she propose that the Enemy held advantage as many times as Sacred Flame?'. Dawn was implicated as a possible double agent when she was seen being dined by two different men on different dates. One of the men, Dong, a much younger academic who said that he desperately wanted to be with Dawn was found to have relatives over the border. His protestations that everyone in Sacred Flame was related directly or indirectly to Enemy residents was met with ridicule in the popular press. His refusal to back down on his assertion that he could verify his claim with demographic data led to his trial and conviction for aiding and abetting the Enemy.

Dong used his time in prison to develop the theoretical basis of what became the Total Eradicator. By the time he was released, Total Eradicator was being seen as the most likely means by which to break the military stalemate. Jan and Dawn were nearing the age of retirement. Candidate replacement historians entered the keen competition for the valued posts and Jan and Dawn were asked for their opinions of each candidate's suitability for office. Jan requested that all should answer one question at interview: 'Will Total Eradicator end or conflate the war?'

Every candidate had a similar answer: either Sacred Flame would conquer Enemy before Enemy could develop the Eradicator or the Enemy would destroy Sacred Flame by winning the development race. Dong, however, had earned his place as a candidate. He had learnt much about history from his devotion to Dawn but, independently, had revolutionized military strategy with his Total Eradicator breakthrough. He sat quietly in the Sacred Flame antechamber with Dawn and Jan Jumbly to explain why the question was ill-conceived.

"There will be a moment, as Jan has shown, when the leap-frogging produces an instant of equality. It is at that moment of balance when each side's Artificial Intelligence Decision-maker will insist that Eradicators be launched before the other side gains an advantage. At that moment, and only at that moment, will it be worthwhile to launch the Deflector. There is only one person able to accomplish this, and it can only be undertaken once. I estimate that the point of equilibrium will occur in exactly one minute from now. Both Eradicators will be launched automatically and, unless protected by the Deflector, all human life – Sacred Flame or Enemy – will be wiped out."

Jan and Dawn looked at one another.

"Are we about to die?" Jan asked.

"No. The Deflector's range will cover this room," Dong responded. "So, if you don't mind, I'll launch it now."

It seemed to Jan, as her heart began to beat uncontrollably, that an awful darkness and silence reigned. Dawn watched Dong as he extracted what looked like a luminous spoon from his inside jacket pocket. He tapped it twice on his nose then held it up and tapped both Dawn's and Jan's nose very lightly. Suddenly there was a rush of wind against the high windows followed by a breathless calm. All three listened, hoping to hear Sacred Flame workers going about their business. But the uncanny quiet persisted. Gingerly, the three of them crept from the room and out into the courtyard. In an unheard-of sacrilege, the Sacred Flame had been extinguished. The tv babbler screens on the streets flickered without a picture whilst emitting a faint white noise.

Over the coming week, Dong, Jan, and Dawn discovered that there were no Enemy combatants: all had died at the same instant as their Sacred Flame compatriots. All that the two remaining official historians were left to accomplish was their account of the war to end all wars. Dong read Jan's thesis, then Dawn's, and his opinion swayed between the two, first one way, then the other.

38

TATTOO

Planning the biggest tattoo convention since the second World War was difficult. Leading American tattooists wanted it in New York, but we had strong representation from European artists who pressed for Paris, Berlin, or Amsterdam. London was the compromise. Central to the convention was our wish to demonstrate the vast history of tattoo practice throughout the world to visitors who may have known nothing about the art. We were proud to have Samoan artists who used wide combs and an assortment of traditional tools made from animal bones. A popular entertainer was the tattooist from Ghana whose depiction of wild animals was greatly admired. The precision of the leading artists from the east coast of the USA and the imagination of the conceptual designs by Italian and French artists attracted the attention of leading art critics who would normally have been seen patrolling national art galleries.

The controversy caused by the challenge thrown down by the Americans was totally unforeseen. Viewing the complexity of the designs from Africa, the Pacific islands, and Europe, they questioned whether these artists could produce the volume required by a growing market. "Precision and simplicity should be our watchwords!" one declared.

We decided that, rather than avoid a dispute and any bad feeling, we should issue a challenge. We asked representatives of every tradition who could demonstrate the greatest number of public recipients of their work. We would award a $5000 prize to the winner.

The next day, an old man, Chaim, walked into the convention and pointed out that whilst tattoos were acceptable in many cultures as well as in the aristocracy and working classes of England where the convention happened to be located, there were some cultures where this was regarded as reprehensible. "If you are a practicing Jew, you would know that tattoos are explicitly prohibited in Leviticus."

This was all news to us, but we could not see what relevance this had to our challenge. It was then that Chaim declared that, despite the prohibition from his religion, he had decided that it was time for him to come forward and claim the prize. He addressed the slowly growing gathering who had come to see the competition that tattoos had been used in ancient China, Persia, Greece, and Rome to mark slaves, prisoners, and criminals. He said he believed that he had been an unwilling practitioner in this tradition.

The Boston artist who was convinced that his record of

6,000 clients could never be exceeded blanched when he realised Chaim's identity.

"When the former tattooist died in 1940, I was only nineteen but took over his job and, with one other survivor, tattooed over 600,000 Auschwitz inmates."

It felt morally wrong to hand over $5,000 to the man who had been part of the Nazi killing machine. But Chaim had also been a child prisoner so, maybe, he deserved recognition for his survival record.

39

THE APPEARANCE OF THE CROCODILE

Serena Sweet was dead. Of course, that was not her real name - but every bookshop had the latest Serena Sweet best-seller in the front window. I was given the investigation as the circumstances of her death were suspicious.

I went to her home. Of course, this was not her real home - just a house she had rented for the summer. I ordered the camera crews and onlookers away from the immediate surroundings.

Her partner had raised the alarm. Of course, he was not her real partner - just the man with whom she had been living that year. He told me he had been unable to get into the locked room and became anxious when she failed to respond to his shouts.

I looked at her computer screen to see if she had left a suicide note. Of course, this was not a notepad - it was the stage for her inventions, her writings, her imaginings.

The last thing she had written was a short story.

I read the story. Of course, I was uncertain whether it was a story, or a report, or a fantasy. It spoke of the appearance of a massive, writhing crocodile in her room. I asked if she had a psychiatric history of paranoid delusions.

I talked to the Medical Examiner. Of course, he could not be sure of the cause of death until a full post-mortem weas carried out. But he did point to what appeared to be the remains of her neck, gouged by enormous teeth marks.

40

THE BLACKSMITH

You could not help but notice that he walked with a huge limp. This was no temporary injury. It was a permanent feature as if one leg was too short or there was a major issue with a broken femur or knee or ankle fusion. He filled the doorway as he entered: a huge, bull-chested figure who slowly made his unsteady way across to the counter.

"I need a large hammer," he said.

"You mean a sledgehammer?" I asked.

"That will do," he replied, "although ideally I would prefer a post maul."

I had never heard of a post maul: but I was embarrassed to display my ignorance.

"I do not think we stock post mauls."

"That's okay. Just let me have the sledgehammer you stock with the longest handle."

Tom, my assistant, sprang into action, promising to bring the customer what he wanted from the storeroom. While we waited for his return, I asked the big man about his purchase.

"If you don't mind my asking, but no one has ever asked me for a post maul. I just wondered what you would want with it and why a sledgehammer comes in a poor second."

"I work in a forge, and we use many different hammers for different jobs. My post maul broke last week, and I really wanted a replacement. But provided it has a long handle, I am sure I can manage with a sledgehammer."

"I did not know we had a forge operating locally. Are you a blacksmith?"

"I work with all sorts of metals. Iron and steel are the most common but, more recently, I have had orders involving much rarer metals like titanium, chromium and even tungsten.

"Your forge must be very well equipped," I said, trying to coax more information from the stranger.

"It is very high-tech," he responded. "We even have a diamond anvil cell."

I was now even more lost than when he referred to a post maul, but I thought I could not avoid showing my ignorance this time. "What is a diamond anvil cell? I am sure we don't sell them."

He smiled and nodded. "No, you certainly won't sell a DAC. We use it to recreate the pressures that you would only find miles underground. That is where the pressures are so great that unusual material like lonsdaleite can be produced."

"So, what is special about lonsdaleite?"

"It's over fifty percent harder than diamond."

"What on earth would you want with a material like that?"

"I have no idea," he said. "We just receive the orders and provide what is requested. How it is used is up to the customer."

"Who could possibly place an order like that?"

"I don't think I am allowed to give out information about customers."

At that moment, Tom reappeared carrying a long-handled sledgehammer.

"That's perfect. I'll take that."

He grasped the hammer with one hand and swung it easily over his shoulder. He limped slowly to the till, paid the bill, and pushed his way out of the doorway – an imposing giant carrying what looked like a massive weapon and terrorizing a couple who were about to enter the store.

I went over to the till and asked to see the payment slip. I was curious about this man's identity but discovered nothing because he had paid with cash.

Tom always struck me as a bit of a nerd. He would spend hours researching whatever interests he was entertaining at the time, investigating everything on the Internet.

"Have you heard of lonsdaleite?" I asked.

He shook his head. "Is it a video game?"

"It is something the guy we just sold the hammer makes in his forge."

Tom walked to the desk with his online laptop and typed in a few enquiries. He showed me entries that confirmed what our customer has claimed about the strange material but gave no indication for what it could be used.

While the frightened customers were being served, I knew that we were no wiser about the identity of the man nor what he was producing in the forge about which we knew nothing. I felt uncomfortable about this but did not know why. It was not as if the man was behaving strangely. He was not demanding a weapon unless you counted the sledgehammer as a weapon. He claimed he needed it for his forge, and, in truth, that is exactly where I would have thought a long-handled sledgehammer might be used. But I knew of no forge in the area. Perhaps he was passing through and was on his way to his forge in another area, or even another country. But after he had limped out, I heard no car or motorbike start up. I imagined that wherever he was heading, he would be walking ... slowly.

I had never done this before ... I mean stalking a customer. But I was more than curious about this strange man and asked Tom to take over the counter whilst I just "popped out for a moment". Out of the store, I easily spotted my lame target on the other side of the street. He was not looking my way, so I decided to walk slowly in his direction but keep to the opposite side of the road. He turned at the corner which forced me to cross over to follow. As I tentatively rounded the corner, I was surprised to see him standing outside the old hotel talking with an extremely beautiful, young woman. She was remonstrating with him, but I could not hear what they were saying. After a minute, they walked into the hotel, and I decided that I would risk discovery by following.

The woman was sitting with her legs crossed on one side of a glass table with the man sitting, hunched, opposite her. She was wearing a long, fashionable dress with a simple pattern that emphasized her attractiveness. She sported long, black hair that shone in the sunlight that flickered through the dusty, hotel windows. Her manicured hands were gesticulating as she spoke. Her high cheek boned face contrasted sharply with the man's who could have been a boxer or prize fighter with his wide, flat face and nose that may have been broken many times. There were several glass tables in the foyer, so I sauntered over to one nearest the couple. I sat with my back to the customer but his partner, facing him, was speaking and I could just about make out what she was saying.

"Your schedule is falling behind," she spoke accusingly.

I could not hear his reply.

"That is a poor excuse. Some of these contracts are time critical."

Again, his response was inaudible.

"You have until the end of the month. My advice is to spend less time on your blacksmith hobby and more on what we pay you for."

He made a comment that did not sound particularly complimentary as he got up to go. He walked towards the hotel entrance. I started to shift my body to stand up and follow him when I felt a hand on my shoulder. I looked up and the young woman said: "Not so fast. I need to talk to you." And she pushed me firmly back into the seat.

She sat opposite me and surveyed me carefully. Then she spoke softly.

"You are not a very good spy, are you?"

I frowned as if to pretend I did not understand.

"You were so obviously tailing him from your store that your performance would have been an embarrassment to any professional espionage agency. I suspect that you are as likely to be in the employment of our enemies as you are to be a research scientist or blacksmith."

"Who are you?" I asked tentatively.

"I am working on your side to protect you and all your friends and customers, your family and even your competitors. You need our protection as enemies are developing and have already developed quite advanced weaponry. They are not afraid to deploy what they have unless they believe we have something of equal or greater potency. And that is where our armourer comes in. The man you followed is our very best armourer."

"But he said he worked in a forge and needed a sledgehammer."

"We are happy to let him continue with his hobbies. But only if he does what we pay him for. And we do not want any local, amateur investigator distracting him. Do you understand?"

I was thinking on my feet. I did not like the way she spoke to me, but she had surprised me, and I was unsure whether she was spinning a yarn or telling the truth.

"I can't help noticing that you have not answered my question. I asked who you were and all I got was a load of bullshit about warfare and the lame man's role in supplying you with weapons."

"You don't really want to know who I am."

"Oh! I do. I would like to the opportunity to assess whether my customer is a blacksmith or an arms dealer."

"He is both. And I am simply his very best client. He will do anything for me."

I looked at her carefully. Slightly coquettish and with her mouth pouting a little as she answered: I discerned that he may have had more interest in her than just a source of income.

"So, the two of you have some history."

She looked at me as if to warn me not to dig too deeply. But I have always reacted badly to anyone keeping secrets from me.

"I can see by the way that he responded to you that you have some sort of hold over him. I cannot believe that this is merely because you pay him for items he creates at his forge."

She took a deep breath. "A few years ago, someone we both knew told him that I was coming to him so that we could become lovers. This was a lie, but neither he nor I knew about it. The misunderstanding led to his naïve attempt to toss me onto one of the couches that surround his forge. He did not know that I was, and still am, the chief self-defense teacher for the espionage teams. I did not mean to break his leg when I threw him over the couch, but he landed heavily on an anvil. He will never fully recover his ability to walk but the person who lied to him will never recover – full stop."

"Where is his forge? I don't know of any locally."

"You ask too many questions, my friend. But you will never discover the forge unless you change your profession and become an arms dealer."

I nearly laughed at his suggestion. But she continued as she rose to go.

"I suggest that you return to your store as Tom will not be able to cope on his own for long. I must return to my home now and I do not believe we will ever meet again ... unless, of course, you come to live near my temple in Athens."

She walked gracefully but quickly out of the building. I clambered to my feet intent upon following but, when I got out the door onto the street, she was nowhere to be seen.

41

THE PERFECT CRIME

It is often said that the wrongdoings of a father introduce the son into a life of crime. Yet that seems to be a pathetic and almost irrelevant observation when considering the extraordinary life of Evelyn Shah.

Even as a child, his preference for dressing as a girl made him a figure of fun. But as he aged, those around him altogether forgot his gender and he was eventually treated as a young woman. Indeed, Evelyn behaved as any young woman would except when it came to dating. Known as a studious and serious young woman without attachments of any sort, she (and perhaps it would be more truthful to use the feminine pronoun for this part of his/her life) became a highly successful accountant and financial executive.

No one knows whether Evelyn concocted her extraordinary parallel lives when very young. What we now know is that whilst she worked her way up as a valued and highly effective bank director during the week, her weekends were not spent in the city. Without any urban attachments (nor even any notable friends), she disappeared onto a train every Friday night and reappeared on the coast – as a man!

By the seaside, Evelyn (or Richard as his landlady knew him) led a totally different life. It is here that he kept his viola where he played in a string quartet with retired professional musicians. His fellow musicians knew him as a cultured performer who never seemed to be short of money. They reported years later that Richard never indicated that he was a high salary earner – only that he had "just enough to get by". Then, on Sunday evening, he would catch the train back to the city and reappear as Evelyn, ready for the world of high finance.

Evelyn's father was a petty criminal whose wife had understandably abandoned him when Evelyn was still at school. Often caught and always impecunious, the father spent as much time behind bars as in the impersonal terrace house, Evelyn's childhood home. It was only after the father's funeral that Evelyn finally enacted the *coup de grâce* which almost destroyed the ancient and internationally established bank from which s/he had extracted most of its liquid assets. By the time that the directors realised what had happened, Evelyn had disappeared, and all the money had gone.

Richard's landlady was delighted that he was finally able to stay in the lodgings for weekdays as well as weekends. The extra cash was most welcome and even his fellow musicians were happy to come and rehearse in his rooms. The landlady liked to hear them play and assumed that Richard had decided to retire from whatever little job used to keep him up in the city. Evelyn had managed to separate his two characters in every possible way. Evelyn's documentation and paltry personal accounts in the city had been abandoned and left in the childhood terrace house. When the police raided it, they found absolutely no indication of Richard's existence.

Because of the size of the robbery, it was almost impossible to keep it out of the public eye. Unlike most organized crime activity where large numbers of men and women are involved together with leading public figures giving their enterprises the appearance of respectability, Evelyn's crime had been committed without any obvious collaborators although it seems probable that the support of at least two untraceable hackers abroad had been enlisted. The sheer scale of his crime made most organized crime syndicates appear little more than petty theft gangs. He had managed in one highly focused hour to redirect the liquid assets of not only those of his employer, but also a great deal of those held in other banks in various tax havens on behalf of criminal gangs and extremely wealthy individuals whom he had tracked from China, Russia, the USA, and the Middle East. It was, and remains, the most phenomenal multitrillion dollar fraud ever committed. Even today, after years of forensic audit and World Bank attempts to track all unusual transactions, none of the money has ever been recovered.

There are a variety of theories about how Evelyn/Richard managed to hide the proceeds of the gigantic robbery. The current favorite is that s/he distributed the money into millions of previously set up accounts all over the world into which comparatively small sums were deposited, which evaded detection because of their tiny size and anonymity. Other notions included the use of accounts that were set up in countries with no reason to be open to international crime prevention authorities; the use of many accounts all of which switched their funds to one another every few seconds; and, most oddly, dumping the assets into what has been described as a 'trough' (an electronic means by which to permanently destroy whatever is dumped there). It is possible that a combination of any of these strategies was used; it is likely that we will never know.

We have some details about Richard's later life. His string quartet began to perform regular concerts in the bandstand above the cliffs. His easy access to cash ensured that the musicians were paid for their appearance and the concerts were lavishly publicized throughout the town. Within a couple of years, the daringly named 'Flight Quartet' was attracting audiences from as far away as the city. Richard probably recognized some of his former bank colleagues in the audience but they, of course, had no notion that Richard, the violist, was their Evelyn.

Some commentators about the greatest thief of our, and any other, time have wondered whether the untouchable funds might have been used for a better purpose. Perhaps s/he might have directed some of the money into worthwhile charitable organizations. Maybe s/he might have been tempted to spend some on himself – maybe a round-the-world trip or a vacation to a resort beside a more attractive sea. But, to our knowledge, the only direct beneficiary of the multitrillion dollar theft was the Flight String Quartet.

One theory that I pursued as a journalist after Evelyn's early death was that s/he had steadily built up a vast portfolio of shares held under different names, until s/he became the effective owner of several major corporations. Using this power, s/he influenced these giant companies to move towards increasingly 'green' investments. My detractors suggest that I see the world through rose-colored spectacles and that Evelyn's influence, if any, might have been in the opposite direction, increasing profits through investments providing the highest returns. Nothing in the unpublished notebook indicates any pecuniary motivation nor interests beyond performing the string quartets of Mozart, Beethoven, Schubert, and Brahms.

Evelyn's early death has been the wellspring of more conspiracy theories than any since the assassination of President Kennedy. The coroner's report named Evelyn as Richard and noted that although anatomically male, and outwardly dressed as such, was clothed entirely with female undergarments. The sparsely maintained room into which the well-paid landlady never ventured revealed nothing except a safe deposit box key in the bedside cupboard drawer. Without any obvious next-of-kin, the box in the local bank was opened by a senior Council officer, accompanied by the police and the bank manager. They found a carefully kept logbook or diary, written in beautiful calligraphy, that recorded the life and matters of importance to the deceased. He obviously did not regard what he had accomplished in theft of particular interest as it is described in the vaguest terms. By contrast, there are pages written about how the Flight Quartet went about preparing for their concerts and miniscule observations about how different bowings and dynamics would affect their interpretation of the masterpieces.

His fall from the cliff has been recorded as an accident. But since the revelations from his logbook, the question remains as to whether he was pushed. After all, there were many powerful organizations that lost vast sums of money on Evelyn's last day at the City Bank. But there were no clues about the circumstances surrounding the fall, only the discovery of the body in the early morning following a particularly fine (and certainly final) concert given by the Flight Quartet in the Cliff Pavilion. His landlady, a regular member of the audience, summed up what she felt after the funeral. "He always played well and always paid well, I shall greatly miss him."

42

THE TRANSMIGRATION

It was an unexpected privilege to be asked to interview Kwan Yin. Since her withdrawal from the spotlight of the world's media, she had shunned contact with journalists like me. So, I was intrigued as to the reason why I had been invited to visit her in the Buddhist community at the foothills of the Himalayas.

On my way, I re-read many of the articles about the most famous woman on the planet. Her mysterious birth was dated from the day that the monks found her deposited on their doorstep and the failure of subsequent investigators to gain even a clue as to who her parents might be. I read about her sheltered childhood and precocious academic abilities that were overshadowed by her amazing physical growth into the seven-foot giantess who could outrun any male. There were plenty of photographs that covered the extraordinary Delhi Olympic Games where she was granted special dispensation to compete in the men's events. Everyone knows about her exploits there: her breaking of the 9 second 100 meters barrier, her winning gold in the long jump and her unbelievable run finishing nearly a mile ahead of the nearest marathon runner. Drug testing found her totally "clean" and she spoke humbly about her strictly vegetarian diet, her hours of meditation before any event and the unusually slow pulse rate to which so-called experts attributed her achievements.

It was only two years later that it was realised that the breakthroughs in mathematics which promoted the Indian sub-continent into its current leadership role were driven by her work. Publishing her findings under a pseudonym, she tried to avoid the adulation that she saw would be heaped upon her yet again. As a young science reporter, I had asked her how she had come to see through the complex problems that had foxed brilliant minds for generations. Her reply that was printed in most newspapers (the only scoop I have ever had!) was frightening in its simplicity. "I view the problem; I meditate upon why it is problematic; I see why it is no problem when viewed from afar; I come closer and write down the solution as I see it."

Her withdrawal back into the Himalayan Sangha at the age of thirty was frustrating for the media hungry for more information about Kwan Yin. But the community protected her privacy, and it was only twenty-five years later that she agreed to an interview and specified that she would only speak to me. Her appearance was a shock. Still standing a full head and shoulders taller than I am, she gracefully shook my hand and asked me to sit beside her. Her hair was still jet black and hung down to her waist, just as it had done as she streaked across the racetrack thirty years before. She smiled and I was disorientated for a moment as she seemed to me to be exactly as I remembered her when she had described her method for solving mathematics problems.

"So, what have you been doing with yourself since I last saw you?" I asked in a weak attempt to open the conversation.

She surveyed me quietly. "My first duties were to care for my children."

"You have children?!" I was so surprised that I nearly leapt from my seat.

"Yes, I have twin boys."

"And are they here in the sangha?"

"No. They prefer to keep quiet about their mother; so, you may not know them. But one went into business and is already one of the wealthiest men in India. The other is a leading practitioner of martial arts. I am most proud of them. But now they have gone. Our children are only on loan and mine have now happily returned to the world."

"Have you continued with your meditation? Have you gained any further insights that you might share?"

She suddenly looked sad. "I feel I have failed in this life," she intoned. "I have not attained bodhi and now believe that this may not be possible."

I immediately realised that Kwan Yin's aspirations towards enlightenment had drained her of much energy. I felt that she perhaps wanted some sort of encouragement from me – a mere journalist but an 'outsider' who may be able to say things that those within her community might not.

"I thought that Buddha only achieved enlightenment after he felt that this might not be possible. Perhaps you are at that stage in your pathway and that nirvana is still attainable. After all, it was for him."

Her head dropped. "It is that achievement for which we all long, the escape from the eternal return, the reincarnations from which we desire a way out. But I now know that my soul will transmigrate and, indeed, I do not believe that any souls have ever escaped."

"Surely you cannot believe that. Buddha himself showed us that this is possible."

"Unfortunately, that is not true."

"I don't understand. How could you know that his great soul did not escape and transmigrate?"

"How do you think?" she said as she quietly wept.

43

TRIANGLE

I was asked to write about the notorious film maker, Thomas Frederickson. The editor's invitation was a work of art in itself:

Dear Alison James,

The owner of the journal is totally against asking you to contribute to this month's edition. He knows that your attacks on Frederickson and his political activities, are themselves, the subject of legal action by his team. But the editor is prepared to risk his own career by inviting you to provide a critique of Frederickson's latest film. Are you willing to accept this challenge?

So, I sharpened my imaginary pen even before taking a seat in the theatre to watch the much-vaunted premier of his latest film. Even before it began, the film had been promoted as a kaleidoscopic portrayal of a group of artists whose fame was based less upon their productions and more upon their ways of life. The film techniques used came from the school of Leni Riefenstahl. I was not impressed by the mock hero worship heaped upon the leader of the group. Frederickson obviously identified himself with the man and the poses adopted by the actor portraying this "hero" were from Sergei Eisenstein's palette. I felt I had been tricked into watching this tedious throwback to early twentieth century totalitarian art.

The one truly interesting character played a comparatively minor role. She was the author, Cécile Bordeaux, who had been dismissed from the group as being too "bourgeois". As a result of watching the film that I think I tolerated until the end only because I was being paid to provide a critique, I decided to investigate Cécile Bordeaux in case she had produced anything worthwhile.

I discovered, to my eternal shame, that she was a celebrated biographer of whose work I was embarrassingly ignorant. The list of those whom she had encapsulated in the strange and difficult art of biography was impressive. We all live lives that are multi-dimensional. But with a book it is only possible to perceive through one dimension – the timeline of your reading page after page. Bordeaux seemed to transcend these constraints by careful attention to detail, cross-referenced to what had already appeared in earlier chapters.

I was brought up with a shock when I saw that her latest biography, created without any contact with the subject, was entitled 'Alison James: the ultimate critic.' I began reading and was surprised by the details of my life that she described. Truth be told, I had forgotten some of them so was intrigued to have them recalled in such excellent prose. The final chapter concluded with an astonishing critical analysis of the Frederickson article I had yet to compose.

44

LEO

This is the story of Leo. At least, that is how I knew him mostly. Others have told me that his gender was uncertain and that some knew him as Leonie when he dressed as a woman. However, I have never considered this an issue of interest although others have tried to assert that this was a critical factor in Leo's life and the decisions and discoveries that are attributed to him.

Leo's father, Xavier, was a celebrated cleric. Whether he was a leading Islamic scholar or Christian teacher is a matter of debate. Categorizing him into these religious pigeonholes seems to me to be of purely academic interest. His impact upon philosophical theory, as well as his influence over Leo, does not require an easy placement within established schools of thought. I have always found his followers' desperate grasp of his best-known aphorism rarely follows a further under-standing of its meaning. 'Without water, there could be no tree, and without tree, there could be no crucifixion' seems to have been best understood by Leo.

Xavier was working in the era of the Autocrats. This was not his choice: he just happened to have been born in the wealthiest nation where it was considered heretical to poke fun at the political leadership. I was in the audience when the most controversial film show was raided by the police, and I found myself in a cell for a couple of days with Leo. The film 'MAGA' was a remake of the old 'Planet of the Apes' movie where the oppressive, armed enforcers were called the 'Monkeys And Gorillas Authority' – much to the chagrin of the actual President. The filmmaker was my talented twin sister, Artemis. But it was the record of Leo's attendance at this show which, later, influenced critical decisions about his true political allegiances.

I will admit that my own feelings regarding patriotism are ambiguous. Like everyone else whom we knew at college and beyond, it was the ideals of democracy, liberty, social equality, and other principles of the Enlightenment to which we aspired. However, as there seemed to be nowhere in this world where these ideals were practiced, alternative commitments were made in order to survive in the actual world in which we lived. Artemis was hounded out of the country and went to live in Norway. My exile from MAGA land is of marginal importance to the story of Leo: but his deportation to the other great Autocracy was a critical moment in this century's evolution.

My work as an image recognition scientist was of minor significance, but the projects upon which I and hundreds of others worked were important. Leo's saw the development of 'merones' as a logical follow-through from understanding Xavier's saying. The conceptualization of what I naively thought of as deep structures that pervaded the Universe which could be accessed even at molecular level was what Leo explained lay behind his father's thinking. Xavier wrote about these universal structures (he regarded the Cross as one) rather like Jung wrote about archetypes that pervade the dream world of people from differing cultures. Each of us casts our own image structures onto the molecular environment within which we live. The manipulation of what we cast by invading this personal space offered an entirely new set of weaponry. 'Merones' (an abbreviation of Molecular Drones) offered a tempting means by which to influence or even assassinate an opponent.

The initial attempts to assassinate President Zed using comparatively crude MAGA merones merely led to the rapid detention of those who had tried flooding the environment with thousands of merones in the hope that one or two would penetrate the defense dome. Zed, in retaliation, tasked his brother Gregory with developing far more powerful merones for a MAGA assault. The laboratory where I was working became a hive of activity attempting to reinforce the dome shields as the race to develop the best defenses became a priority for autocrats on every continent.

Whether it was with or without the permission of his brother, Gregory decided to use merones upon those he regarded as political opponents within the country. He would build various dome structures around them and, if they did not work, then he simply reported their death to a grateful President Zed. But Gregory was not as adept as the MAGA technicians in creating the most lethal merones, nor the means by which to stop them. Some whispered rumors in our laboratories suggested that perhaps Gregory was not averse to the possibility of Zed succumbing to the next attack, leaving the leadership open for him. The prospect of a Gregorian autocracy frightened many of us even more than the notion of a MAGA takeover!

Zed's survival was entirely due to Leo's genius. Much to Gregory's annoyance, Leo evolved an alternative defensive strategy which required a depth of understanding far beyond Gregory's abilities. But Zed would allow no new initiative without the approval of his trusted Head of Security, Krebs. Gregory pestered Krebs to block any suggestions from Leo. "We don't even know if he is Leo or Leonie. And he comes from MAGA land. How can we trust him?" But Krebs watched the video of our being entertained by the Planet of the Apes remake and Leo's subsequent eviction from the land of his birth. If anything, Krebs was more suspicious of Gregory than Leo. So, he allowed Leo to speak directly with the President.

Leo explained to Zed that there would be no defense dome as this would almost certainly be penetrated. Instead, Leo could protect the President if he were allowed to take blood samples from Zed. From these he would construct an entirely fake molecular image of the President. Zed's own image projection would be obscured leaving the fake image open to attack. Sure enough, the MAGA attack saw swarms of merones destroy the fake. MAGA observers knew that the attack had been successful yet, the next day, Zed was more alive than ever.

It was a week after this brilliant coup that I met Leo. He was dressed as Leonie and was dancing in the Dionysus gay club: but Zed's pathological hatred of homosexuality did not extend to closing the club where he knew his saviour would hang out for relaxation. On the contrary, there were several poorly disguised, heavily armed guards surrounding the building in case anyone tried to take down Zed's star scientist. Even Krebs himself could be seen surveying the dancers from a vantage point. Perhaps he would have liked to join the dance?

Of course, Leo did not think of himself as a scientist. Like Xavier, he regarded the intramolecular realm within which he worked and roamed as the visible location of the archetypal structures that underpinned what we perceived as "reality". Others in the club declared themselves convinced by voodoo and other animalist beliefs. But Leo, like his father, refused to follow this well-trodden path. He (or she) talked to me at the bar in the club about how these archetypal structures pervade our dreams as well as what we believe as the 'real world'.

"I loved my father and his delving into the substructure of life opened the way for us to understand the Universe in which we live and die," he said to me. "But you know that those who took his words literally concerning water, wood and the crucifixion are as foolhardy as those who believe in the literal translation of the many holy texts that we are taught. Do you know that the fundamentalists who support the mad MAGA honestly believe that he will live for eternity provided they can erase all water and wood from the intramolecular universe within which they dream. They have gone about destroying all trace of water and wood so that his projected image cannot be crucified!"

"So, what will happen to him?" I asked.

"You will see his fate in a collective dream in the coming month. I am sure." And, with that, Leonie skipped away and started dancing with a graceful man who had, no doubt, been thoroughly checked over by Krebs.

The International Celebration of Xavier's Life and Work was due to take place in Oslo. Brilliant scientists and metaphysicians attended, and Leo was a star speaker. Zed allowed him to go provided he was accompanied by a small army of guards with an array of weaponry usually only on display for the autocrats themselves. Leo left strict instructions with Krebs that no one should be allowed access to Zed without the protective screen that could only be operated from within the President's own private study. Michael Mayer (or MM as he was known) had been one of Xavier's star pupils: but in Oslo he presented a MAGA-based theory that Leo described as absurd. "You fail to grasp Xavier's insight that the crucifixion is primary and that it will find any way by which to become manifest. By deleting water and tree, you simply invite alternative manifestations.

One of MM's fundamentalist followers objected to Leo. "You are just a pawn in Zed's game. You should not be here. You will say anything to deny the possibility that we can achieve eternal life for MAGA. He will not be crucified because we will prevent that fate within the confines of the molecular universe within which we are now the masters."

"That idiot doesn't even understand how immersion into the crucifixion archetype guarantees some form of existence beyond an individual's physical death," Leo commented to his guards who had no idea what Leo was talking about.

Gregory's coordinated assault upon the MAGA presidency was timed to coincide with MM's absence in Oslo. The launch of thousands of merones within the vicinity of the victim was countered by MM's impressive ion dome defense. Over ninety five percent of the merones were destroyed: but the five percent that evaded the ions were more than enough to kill the man. The world's press and social media largely presented this assassination as the response to the attempt upon Zed that had been totally countered by Leo's defense. And, just as Leo predicted, many of the MAGA followers reported a collective dream in which they saw their hero strung up roughly within a latticework of metal scaffold bars – with no wood nor water anywhere to be seen.

Leo's return from Oslo was marred by a crude attempt on his life. The aircraft in which he was travelling was forced to make an emergency landing when a sabotage explosive failed to ignite. Krebs met Leo the moment he arrived home with news that there had been another attempt upon Zed.

"We don't know how the attacker evaded your defensive device. How is it possible?"

Leo surveyed the data sets and pointed to a telltale eruption of figures whose presence was unexpected. "That is an entry into Zed's private molecular space. Whoever made that entry must have planted the disruptor which could kill our leader."

Gregory told Krebs that he suspected Leo. But Krebs knew that Leo had already saved Zed's life once before and, anyway, the attack was carried out when Leo was in Oslo. Zed, feeling very ill, and Krebs, looking very harassed, met with Leo to ask how to identify the intruder.

"That's very simple," Leo asserted. "Present that plume of data that accompanied the intruder upon entry into the identification funnel. It's the same one you use for identifying anyone requesting entry into the palace. You will obtain a clear image of their face and a readout of their DNA. I will bet my last paycheck that it will be the same person who ordered the bomb to be planted in my aircraft coming home."

When Krebs shared the readout with Zed, the president was incandescent with rage. "I knew that Gregory was ambitious: but to want to murder his own flesh and blood!"

The next morning the Dionysus was buzzing. Rumors surged and receded; no one really knew what was happening. It was thought that Gregory had fled the capital and was hiding in one of the ecclesiastical palaces, protected by his close ally, Archbishop Nicholas.

When Leonie arrived, she caused a stir. Dressed in an immaculate silk dress and sporting a voluptuous, blond wig, she came and sat down near our little band of image recognition technicians and scientists. Krebs himself could be seen directing his men to create a protective ring around our table. The archbishop had issued a notice strongly implying that Leo was somehow behind the attempt upon Zed and that the case against Gregory was a foul MAGA slander. Krebs regarded this as a desperate act to save Gregory. After all, as the assault was taking place, thousands of delegates and a massive posse of his own guards were watching Leo perform in Oslo.

"You are looking very beautiful today," I commented to Leonie. She smiled at me, her fellow fugitive from MAGA after the fury created by the Planet of the Apes remake. "Come and dance with me," she said.

Dozens of couples were on the dance floor: but they made way for us. I whispered in her ear: "how did you do it?"

She began pirouetting and suddenly stopping with a jerk to point at the floor behind me. Then she repeated the maneuver but pointed at the floor behind her. I was unsure of what she was trying to say. But after a couple of twists, I realised she was pointing at our shadows.

"Shadow!" I said under my breath.

She nodded and called out a word that sounded like "young" but then I understood she was trying to make me focus upon the word "shadow" within the conceptions laid out by "Jung". She laughed when she saw that I understood but gave no further clues in case others twigged what she was telling me. A few minutes later, she made a dramatic exit, plunging through the back door supported by a small troupe of dancers who had accompanied her throughout the performance.

There was a sudden stir as an announcer entered the club. Normally, governmental announcers only made pronouncements online or via tv and radio. But this one walked to the stage and silence fell across the room.

"A few minutes ago, despite all that our best physicians could do, our beloved leader, President Zed, passed away. No stone will be left unturned to discover how he was killed and the perpetrator will not escape justice. As a sign of respect, this club and the others that opened this morning will be closed until further notice."

As we filed out, I could see Krebs talking to the announcer. He was agitated and gesticulating wildly. I hoped that an unstable Krebs did not spell danger to Leo or any of us whom he might suspect of treachery. Innocence, as we had seen, was no protection against a furious but perplexed security chief. But the truth was that Krebs regarded Leo as the one true, loyal guardian of his leader because of his initial action in diverting the MAGA merone attack. Krebs hated the pontificating archbishop and the fact that Nicholas was shielding the strongest suspect in Zed's death had him pressing the announcer to declare Gregory as the most wanted man on the run.

In the event, Krebs never got his hands on Gregory. Thinking he was safe within the confines of the great cathedral was a sad error of judgement. Known as the driver of the merone attack that had killed the MAGA leader, a revenge assault was made against him by the Michael Mayerson team. He died holding his head and falling back onto the altar, a "sacrificial lamb" according to the archbishop, keen to retain some religious significance to the man's death. But this untimely demise left Krebs with many unanswered questions.

The spectacular dance that Leonie had used to cover what she hoped was a secret message did not fool Krebs. Although he could not understand what was being said, he knew that there had been a message and was determined to discover what it was and what it meant. To mislead an intelligent analyst like Krebs, it was always best to keep as near the truth as possible. I realized that the reference to the Jung archetype, shadow, would have been worked out even before questioning, I hoped I was prepared for the interview carried out by Krebs himself.

"What was Leo telling you in the club?"

"This was Leo's alter ego, Leonie, so she likes working in riddles and artistic poses. But I think I worked out what she was saying on behalf of Leo."

"Well, tell me what she said."

I took a deep breath here and paused. I hoped that this would convince Krebs that I was coming clean about the entire message. I asked for a drink of water and Krebs shouted to one of the guards to bring in a carafe. Once I had taken a sip, I went on with my tale.

"Leonie wanted me to understand the word 'shadow' in a very specific context.

She knew that in my face recognition work I would have had to study all the various theories about underlying structures that usually determine exactly what it is we see. So, she shouted a word that, at first, I thought was 'young'. But that didn't make sense. We know exactly how old Zed and all our leading players are. But then I wondered whether the word she was trying to articulate was 'Jung'. Are you following what I'm saying?"

Krebs nodded and I knew that I had told him nothing that he had not already worked out for himself.

"In Jungian theory, shadow has a very specific meaning. It is an archetype. But its significance alters between people. Shadow for me is not shadow for you. So, what was shadow for Zed? That was the question whose answer would tell us everything that Leo knew."

I paused again because I wanted to gauge how much of this Krebs had already surmised. It seemed to me that this was just as far as he had reached and that my honesty so far should put me in good stead when it came to my interpretation.

"Go on. Don't stop there!" Krebs was becoming excited. This was a good sign.

"My understanding of shadow – and you can check this out with any of our psychologist specialists – is that it is a bit like the contents of Pandora's tin or box. All the fears and troubles that you have are contained therein and it remains as a constant thorn in the mind, pricking away with nowhere else to go. It is an archetype, so it cannot go away. It is a permanent feature of each of our universes. So, what was in Zed's shadow. What was the fear that would never leave him? Whatever it was points to where the attack originated. I think I know what Leo saw as Zed's shadow."

"You can prove this?" Krebs interjected.

I shook my head. "There can be no proof now because even a deep trance analysis of Zed's fears undertaken whilst he was under hypnosis is no longer available to us. But I think that Leo saw Zed's deepest shadow as betrayal."

Krebs and I sat in silence whilst he digested this interpretation. He was thinking about Zed as his boss, as his friend, as the nation's disputed leader and of those who might represent a challenge. Eventually, he nodded.

"I have no idea why Leo has to put on all this make up and female attire. Couldn't he just have told us what you have just told me?"

I shrugged my shoulders. "I'm not a performance artist. I'm just an analyst so I don't really understand how his temperament works. But he is the creative. He is the only one to have evolved the effective defense against merones. He saved Zed against the MAGA threat but could not be here defending Zed against someone so close to him whilst speaking to the rest of the world in Oslo. I know Gregory and the archbishop were accusing Leo of this crime, but I do not believe a word they say.

Krebs nodded. "No. Nor do I. You can go now. Thank you for telling me all you know. Do you think I could discover more from interviewing Leo himself?"

"I'm sure you will try but my only fear is that he will transform into Leonie and annoy you for appearing to be evasive. But you know that, at heart, he is on our side and may have more insight into what our enemies are planning than any of us by dreaming and imagining scenarios that we cannot grasp yet."

--

Krebs was woken up the next morning by a shout from

Leo. He had had the cheek and initiative to visit Krebs at his home before the investigator called him in.

"What do you want?" Krebs was slightly annoyed, but Leo had him on the back foot.

"We need to establish a video link to Michael Mayerson urgently. We can bring this war to a successful conclusion: but only if I can speak directly to Mayerson. I know him well. He will be at a loss what to do next, but I am already a step or two ahead of him."

Krebs was about to object but Leo walked away quickly and shouted: "I'll call you later as I need to prepare now."

That afternoon saw Leo with a very small group of us sitting in a study awaiting the video feed to go live. When it buzzed into life, we could see Mayerson in a huge operations room surrounded by dozens of technicians, security guards, software specialists (some of whom I knew) and psych specialists brought in to advise on how to deal with Leo. Leo sat with just a couple of face recognition people, an interpreter (if needed) and Krebs. He assured us that he could deal with "poor Michael".

Leo had warned Krebs that Mayerson's team would attempt to convince Krebs that Leo was the criminal who had killed his leader. "He will first try to sow division amongst his enemies. You need to pretend to be listening and, eventually, it will be my turn to speak. That is when the meeting proper will begin and we shall see how they react. I suspect that they will be shocked and may even disbelieve what I can do as they have no idea how to manipulate deep molecular structures. But they will have to learn." Krebs nodded and Leo asked me and the other face recognition specialists to watch Mayerson for telltale facial expressions that would guide us in deciding how to deal with him.

The meeting began exactly as Leo had predicted. Mayerson asked Leo how he had managed to murder Zed. "Congratulations, Leo, in pretending to save him one day just so that you would have the opportunity to kill him and Gregory a few days later."

Leo smiled and said he appreciated Michael's professional praise for his achievements but that was not the main reason why we were having the meeting.

"You see, Michael, the question is not how to murder people with merones. What you and I need to agree is how to prevent people being murdered. Otherwise, this tit for tat war could go one forever. I am sure you agree."

Leo looked to us for an assessment as to how Mayerson was reacting. "I think he is unsure. He doesn't know where you are going in this," I whispered in his ear. Leo nodded.

"Now I know that whatever verbal or written assurance I give you, or you give me, will be regarded with skepticism. So, without consulting you or other security focused personnel, I decided to act on my own and believe I may have resolved the problem finally."

"How could you have done that?" a disbelieving security guard sitting beside Mayerson interjected.

"I'm sorry," Leo said, "I don't think I know you. Are you a specialist in molecular deep structures? If not, perhaps you will allow me to talk with Michael Mayerson who is one of the world's experts."

Mayerson pushed the man aside. "What have you done Leo?" he asked.

"It is all a question of which is the appropriate deep structure to engage when an attack is about to take place."

"What do you mean?"

"Well, Michael, I have rearranged the substructure."

"What! How have you done that?"

"An explanation of how my practice has developed so much further will have to wait until later. Meanwhile, let me explain what will happen if anyone attempts any form of merone attack, anywhere in the world against anyone – and that includes people who live here in our country. I have organized the substructure to engage one and only one archetype. You will recognize it as the ouroboros, the snake biting its tail."

Mayerson spun round and started talking with his psych specialists. He was clearly unclear as to what Leo's actions would mean. Eventually, he turned back and said: "My team believe that what you have done is to set up a structured guarantee that anyone launching an attack would be attacking themselves. Is that correct?"

"Your experts are to be congratulated. That is precisely what would happen."

"So, if we launch an assault on you and you take no defensive maneuver, the attacker will be committing suicide."

"Exactly."

"Do you want us to attempt to kill you?"

"Of course not. I am simply saying that if any loyal soldier from your impressive armed forces were to try to kill me with merones, he would die the moment he launched the attack, and I would remain unscathed."

A huge bull of a man in battledress pressed forward, pushing Mayerson aside. He was shouting but until he reached Mayerson's microphone, we could not make out his words. Finally, we heard him scream: "you cannot take this girlie seriously. He dresses in a frock and thinks he can outbluff a soldier. This joker knows damn well that I have an advanced merone contingent surrounding his venue. Now he believes that he can scare us into downing our weapon. But my men on the ground need do nothing as I can launch the fastest merone ever constructed straight at the back of his head, right now."

The tiny, handheld control was slammed onto the table, as if the man believed he had won a high money round of poker. The launch button was banged down and a zip sound screeched through the room. The era of the Autocrats ended with General Trumpington Water's decapitation.

BOOK THREE: THE TZADIK

THE TZADIK AND THE RIVER

I found the famous tzadik standing in nothing but a swim-suit beside the river. I asked him what he was doing: "trying to contemplate the meaning of Ein Sof". I knew enough about the traditions of the Kabbalah to understand that he was meditating upon the endlessness of the Universe. I assumed that this was an essential part of his religious duties but was surprised when he turned and asked me to look hard at the river and describe what I saw.

I spoke about the water running fast towards the far-off sea. He smiled and said: "the water has carved out the land just as all matter in the Universe has carved out space. So, space is nothing other than what matter has created."

I had read books about General Relativity and, although no mathematician, could grasp the concept as described by the tzadik. But I wanted to tax him further as he seemed happy to talk in terms I understood. "So, what is space-time?" I asked.

"Look at the flow," he answered. "In which direction is the water moving? You've heard of the 'arrow of time' so most people believe that is time. So, if I want to identify a single molecule of water, I could give you its co-ordinates by saying it is in the river exactly 100 kilometers before the sea (length ways), 50 meters from the bank (width), 10 meters down (depth) and 2 hours after it set off from the spring from which the river began its journey (time). Does that answer your question?"

I shifted uncomfortably as I could not see why the molecule could not have been identified without any reference to time at all. The tzadik smiled: "That's right. The 'arrow' of time says nothing except the direction in which the water flows. Let me give you a better idea. Imagine that you know absolutely everything about the land that has been carved by the river. Forget the water: you know every detail of the land itself, the mountainside from where the river started, the meanders, the way the delta expands. Now imagine that you are looking across from one bank to the other – not up and down the river – just at one instant of the river's existence. Now tell me, if you knew nothing about how the contents of the basin flowed, how would you know what it was you were seeing? At that moment, were you having a tiny glimpse of water, or was it lava from a volcano? Perhaps it was not matter at all, just a tiny moment in the progress of a beam of light?"

"Surely I could just reach out my hand and tell?"

"Of course, the only way that you can tell what's in the river is by experiencing it in some way. The easiest is by observing how matter proceeds in time: obviously light and water travel at very different speeds. However, you are closer to the truth than you think when you speak of reaching out your hand. You see, it is a pretence that we make when we make "objective observations" as if we were standing on the bank with a set of scientific instruments. In fact, we are all living in the river. We are swept along, and our observations are strongly affected by our constant need to avoid drowning."

"But surely the laws of Physics pertain irrespective of where you or I happen to be in the river?"

"Well, that depends on what you mean by the laws of Physics. The physical existence of the river basin is not constant. If you like, we can say that the way that space-time has been "curved" means that your experience of time in the river will always differ from mine. What you say is 'now' will not seem to me to be 'now'."

"Yes, but the way that matter behaves in the river will still obey certain rules, irrespective of where you or I happen to be located."

"If you mean that the way that matter interacts tells us all about gravity and what we have deduced about the laws of gravity gives us the most powerful possible insight as to how matter behaves, then I agree. But that is only describing certain behaviours within a three- or four-dimensional model of the Universe that we find able to grasp. The problem is that it does not help us understand those aspects in the river that seem to require further dimensions before we reach an understanding."

At this point I was waiting for the tzadik to plunge into a discourse about the Kabbalah where supernatural concepts underpin any description of what we do not understand. But I was pleasantly surprised when he left any religious or quasi-religious explanations aside.

"Now you see, I think, why the notion of time as something that can be reduced to little other than the direction of flow totally fails to provide a fuller understanding of nature. If you start by grasping that the notion of simultaneity is a chimera, then being immersed within the river will make us "see" an electron "here" and "simultaneously" "there". The river clearly exists in three dimensions of space: but it is less obvious why it also exists in three dimensions of time."

"I don't understand," I said. "Why three?"

"Take any object in the stream. We can describe it in terms of three space dimensions: its height, depth, and width. Obviously, its density is just a matter of scale: greater density simply means measuring the contents of what is in its volume. And scientifically minded people like you, my friend, are fascinated by what happens when the density becomes so great that we get black holes: and the way that gravity and matter actually scrape out the structure of the riverbed – the Universe's space is created by matter. But you then simply stick the progression of time as a fourth dimension when all that this does is indicate the direction of flow."

I interjected: "I think it's important to understand how the density and volume of matter impacts upon the movement of other matter. It explains why black holes and other singularities exist."

The tzadik nodded. "But it is useless in explaining how complexity (especially organic) has developed and what are its boundaries. Nor what consciousness is unless some dimension of time (and matter?) exists that is not immediately apparent as you look across the river in that one instant of time. The only way I know how to grasp what we see in our river is by assuming that there are also three dimensions of time. The first is progression: clock time; the "arrow" that simply indicates the direction of flow. The second is velocity: this indicates what proportion of what you are observing is matter and how much is energy. Obviously if the object is a photon, its velocity will be so great that it will have no mass at all. The third is complexity: this measures the sheer amount of internal feedback mechanisms that exist within what you are observing and may tell you whether what you are seeing is alive. None of these attributes are measurable within dimensions of space but, when these three are combined with the three space dimensions, only then can we understand fully what is space-time and what is happening in the river in which we live."

I was struck by the tzadik's self-assurance about what still seemed to me to be fairly unfamiliar reasoning. But, out of mischief, I decided to extend his river analogy in an attempt to have a bit of fun. "I suppose that you can see all this because you are sailing down the river in a boat whilst I'm just trying to learn to swim."

He laughed. "I'm afraid you are accusing the wrong person

of being a sailor. I seem to spend most of my life under-water. Those in the boats hold power and cling to it as they are afraid of falling into the water. Most of them are quite happy carving their way through life carelessly smashing into all the public who are just trying to survive by swimming. But until you made your little joke, I had not thought about the political dimension of the river. Thank you."

And with that the tzadik plunged into the water and was swept around the meander and out of sight.

47

THE TZADIK AND THE CHANNEL

I came across the tzadik again, shuffling away from the river looking despondent.

"What's the matter?" I asked.

"There is nowhere to stand by the river down there. The water flows into a channel with such steep sides that you cannot get near the flow."

"Does that matter?"

"I want you to think about what you cannot see," he replied. "If you cannot get a vantage point, then you cannot know what is happening."

"No, but you can surmise what is occurring can't you?"

"Of course, that is what we do all the time whether we have a vantage point or not. After all, we only have our easily fooled senses to rely on wherever we are. But I was probably looking gloomy as I thought about how attached I was to acquiring a vantage point. It is a vain attachment because it assumes that we can detach ourselves from the river within which we live our lives whereas what we see is largely determined by how we are coping in the flow."

"I understand that. But surely, we can imagine how the river affects us and adjust our perspectives and conclusions accordingly?"

"Well, there is a way of reducing our view of the river as nothing other than a bare riverbed. But we know that that is, itself, a vain concept as the riverbed cannot have come into existence without the river that formed it. Similarly, you can imagine what the river looks like without us being part of it: but that is also a vain concept as our existence is part of that river."

"Hang on," I exclaimed. "Surely, we can surmise what the land looked like before the river ever flowed? It was just flat terrain before the water started to cut into it."

"You might think that" the tzadik said quietly. "But why did the water flow where it did? Do you not think that the terrain itself might have had pre-existing cracks and curves that guided the water course? A land with dips and mounds (I call them de Sitters) and with passes between them (I call them anti-de Sitters). I find the idea of a perfectly flat plain, a Minkowski, a little like the ideas held by those who belonged to the Flat Earth Society." The tzadik was chortling at his own little joke.

I could not share his joke. I told him that I could see no point in wondering about the pre-existing landforms as the water just flowed where it did whatever we might think. But he tutted as if my ignorance annoyed him and said: "You still don't understand, do you? You think that the flow must be water. But if it were lava, then a quite different channel would be cut. And if it is just a stream of light, we would have to think about the concept of flow quite differently. You see it is the density, velocity and complexity of what flows that largely determines what sort of channel is cut."

I reflected for a moment and imagined how dense, fast-moving matter could impact upon its surroundings. But I was struggling to think how matter's complexity could make any difference.

The tzadik read my mind, held out his hands and said: "Look at what this complex web of cybernetic organic material just decided to do – it held out two hands. Complex matter has the capacity to make its own decisions about movement within the boundaries set by our position in the channel created by the river's flow. I think you like to call it free will."

48

THE TZADIK AND THE STONE

The tzadik was kicking a stone and muttering to himself as he walked beside the river. "What's wrong?" I called. He turned and pointed a finger at me. "He is your friend, isn't he?" I asked who he meant, and he gave the name of a distinguished academic who did happen to be a friend.

"What have you got against him?" I asked.

The tzadik glowered and spat out the two letters "A.I." My friend had carried out groundbreaking work in the field of artificial intelligence so I assumed the tzadik was going to roll out the usual criticism of the field questioning whether any machine could ever match human intelligence.

"Your friend was trying to convince me that as the brain receives information, processes it and then decides on action; then this is what our most sophisticated computers do. He obviously believes that once our machines have mastered all the neural processes and can replicate them, then we can have a genuinely intelligent product that is not human but can match us."

"Well, that seems to be a rational viewpoint. Of course it doesn't answer fundamental questions about what consciousness is: but surely it will do as a working model?"

The tzadik picked up the stone he had been kicking. He tossed it into the air, and it landed further down the path. "Did you see that?" he asked. "It was on the ground, it was launched into the air, and then it landed safely further away. So, does that make it a useful model to explain the aircraft industry? After all that's all aircraft do. Your friend and his colleagues are doing the equivalent of demanding that we analyze consciousness by experimenting with circuitry. We may as well attempt to analyze the aircraft industry by experimenting with stone throwing. I am cross because he and his ilk are wasting vast sums of money and effort in a pointless exercise that does nothing other than help us throw stones further."

The tzadik walked off, kicking the stone into the river with a farewell curse.

49

THE TZADIK AND CHOICE

I came across the tzadik beside the waterfall. He saw me and smiled.

"What are you doing?" he asked.

"I was looking for you," I replied. "I have some important choices to make soon and could do with your advice."

"Look at the waterfall," the tzadik exclaimed. "There was a man who set out in his boat, full of confidence. It had a powerful outboard motor, and he was a most experienced captain. The river ran swiftly as there had been a lot of rain over the past few weeks. But his journey should not have been remarkable. He had ploughed his way to the far bank many times."

"The man had an exceptionally precious cargo covered in a tarpaulin roped around it to keep it dry. The roar of the motor had a reassuring effect as he started up-stream. But when he reached the very center of the current, there was a vomiting sound that he had never heard before. For a moment, he thought it might be the screech of some big bird flying overhead. But there was no shadow falling across his bows from above. As the motor fell silent, he took a sharp and involuntary intake of breath."

I nodded but the tzadik paused. After a while he continued.

"The man pulled on the cord to start the engine again but then realised why it would not respond. The fuel tank had run dry. In amongst the precious cargo, he knew that there was a small refill bottle. But the river would not wait. It had already caught hold of the boat and was sweeping it back beyond his point of departure... towards the waterfall."

"Now the man had to make an important choice. Just for a moment he sat perfectly still. It was as if he were at the fulcrum of a great and ungainly machine that swung about in a vain attempt to discover its point of balance. And, inadvertently, he had found it. And he could see his choices with absolute clarity as if they had always been there engraved in stone. He could burrow into the cargo in search of the refill. At the speed the boat was travelling and the way it had started to rock and spin, he knew that this would mean losing cargo overboard as he would have to loosen the security moorings. And at the end, if he failed to restart the engine in time, he and the boat would be hurled down the waterfall. On the other hand, he could abandon the boat and cargo now. He could slip into the water and swim towards the shore. He was a reasonable swimmer and would normally expect to reach safety; but with the speed of the current, he had doubts as to whether he could make it. And the boat with all its precious cargo would be lost."

"Being a lateral thinker, he also considered two unusual alternatives. Prayer had not been a habitual activity although he could see that the appearance of divine intervention at this moment would be opportune. Supernatural occurrences would, he was sure, take the appearance of a natural event that was extremely unexpected. Perhaps the river would suddenly part because of an avalanche of rock released by the recent heavy rain. The temporary dam would allow him to step from the boat, lift the most precious of the cargo clear, and walk to dry land. Or maybe a sudden drop in temperature would freeze the river just before he reached the waterfall."

"The other alternative occurred to him as he contemplated the arc the boat would take as it took the plunge. It would hit the rocks beneath and disintegrate on impact. The debris, the remains of the cargo and his body would be washed up on the little beach as the river meandered away immediately after the waterfall. But the arc would be quite different if he could position the boat in the very center of the current. It would be launched into the air at greater speed. And maybe, just maybe, it would clear the rocks and arrive, flat-bottomed before the beach. The boat may remain intact, though damaged. The cargo could be saved. He should expect injury but could escape with his life. He reflected on this course of action and realised that, although a possibility worth considering in the circumstances, the likelihood of success was very slight."

"He thought about prayer again. Unprompted, he asked himself what would God do when faced with such choice?

The answer was obvious and easy for a divinity. Slipping off the boat and deserting the boat and cargo still left the option of re-creating everything at a later date. When the Great Flood subsided, God was still there to start again. But his cargo had taken a lifetime to bring together. He would not be able to do it again."

"He considered the nature of choice. What would be the effects of any decision that he made? Could the choice of action give meaning beyond anything that he might intend? When God decided to elect a Chosen People, His own precious cargo, were their sufferings determined by that choice? Should he let go of his cargo and let everything that he had worked for slip, unobtrusively, into history? Surely others, more worthy than him, could pick up the torch where he had dropped it?"

The tzadik asked: "What would you do in that situation? Risk is not just a calculation of probabilities, you see. It is more a question of character."

"Tell me what the man does in your story."

"Come now. It is you who are looking for advice about choice. So, what would you do?" he asked. I tried to imagine myself in the predicament. It seemed obvious that the most obvious choices would be unlikely to succeed.

"I think I would tear the tarpaulin off, rope two corners to my feet, seize the rope at the other two corners in my hands and launch myself over the fall and try to abseil down."

The tzadik smiled approvingly. "You do not appear to need any advice concerning choice." Then he added: "Unfortunately the captain reacted like most people. As he dug into the cargo, he framed the image of the refill bottle in his mind and tried to picture exactly where it would be. He did not have time to look up to see the great bird flying across the river, throwing its long shadow across his bows."

50

THE TZADIK AND DURATION

I came across the tzadik very slowly pacing along the towpath. Then quite suddenly he burst into a fast walk then lurched to a halt.

"What on earth are you doing?" I called.

He looked up surprised to see me. He mumbled something to himself as if slightly ashamed of having been discovered behaving oddly. I smiled and decided I was not going to let him pretend that nothing had happened.

"Come on. Don't mumble. Just tell me what you think you were doing," I demanded.

He took a deep breath, looked me in the eye, and said "I was trying to assess what effect my movement would have on my sense of time."

"By sense of time, I suppose you mean what I might call duration."

"Quite right. But what if duration was simply our perception of what time was in reality? If matter itself generates space-time, then presumably different forms of matter might generate a variety of temporal realities. So, duration might be what happens to the dimension of time when it interacts with organic material. Life itself could be "bending" time."

"So, what were you doing just now?"

"I was seeing if I sensed time differently when I moved at different velocities. But, of course, that was being silly as if there was any "bending" going on, it would be so miniscule that there is no way that I could measure it just by thinking about what was happening as I walked."

And with that, he walked gingerly up the towpath casting a careful eye across the river as it rushed past him.

51

THE TZADIK AND TIME

I had hoped to hear more of what the tzadik might say about time: but he disappeared soon after I taxed him about what I thought would be an easy discussion. How wrong I was!

"You must have a view on how we perceive time." I said as we met on the sandy ground near the river. But he looked at me as if I had struck him.

I began to apologize, worrying if I had unintentionally offended him. But he sat down and started to speak as if I were not there. I shall try to summarize what he said as best as I can remember it.

"We perceive the Universe through our senses, but our senses are also part of that Universe. The medium through which that sensing occurs we speak of, in a crude reduction, as "time".

For simplicity's sake we shall call that time-framed

relationship we build up as our "mind". But, over the centuries, our minds have evolved in ways that can only be understood if we understand more about time.

Some people's time perception is similar to a film projection. It is made up of a myriad of static images that flicker past at different rates, depending upon our age, our mental state (that could be affected by drugs or some other chemical or biological factor) and fatigue. These people see the world in a very different way from those who perceive it as a flow, like a river. So those who feel time as a series of states – a view of time as a series of static existences – are quite different to those who perceive the Universe as processive."

The Tzadik paused to see if I was following and, once I assured him, that I was with him, he continued. "Now here is a harder concept for you. There are those who take what we might call a passive view of the Universe as opposed to those whose relationship is felt to be active. The reason why this is a harder concept to grasp is because you need to understand that time itself, in the Universe and, of course, in our own brains and bodies, is not what we have simplified with clocks. At a quantum level, we are able to glimpse the way that time itself wavers forwards and backwards so that particles can appear to be in two places at the same time – but, of course, "the same time" means very little once we can accept time as "shivering"

(*Ed note: I think the Tzadik might have said "shimmering"*)."

The tzadik paused and laughed to himself. When he saw my puzzled look, he made a comment about which I understood nothing but went something like: "Penrose and Hammeroff were onto something but failed to grasp that it is the Universe itself that shivers (*shimmers?*) and our brains simply register this as they are part of that movement back and forth." I asked what he meant but he just continued without explaining his little comment to himself.

"I am going to draw a few simple lines on the sand here." And as the tzadik drew a little diagram, he began to explain.

"I want you to think of those whose minds are orientated to a more passive perception of the World as having brains that tend to coalesce around what might be described (in clock terms) as an earlier temporal view. Those with a more active perception seem to project forward with a view that has features that appear to be later. Of course, these "earlier and later" notions are only describable by scientists as ridiculously simplified features of quantum mechanics. But no matter! You will see what I mean when I draw."

MIND	PROCESSIVE time perception	STATIC time perception
ACTIVE/ CHANGE stance towards universe	PRESENT	FUTURE
PASSIVE/ ACCEPTING/ BEING CHANGED stance towards universe	PAST	TIMELESS

"You see, those with an active perception who see time as processive tend to have a present time orientation. Active and static: future time orientation. Passive/processive: past time orientation. Passive and static: timeless."

Speaking with some feeling, he went on: "I am regarded as a tzadik, so people believe I hold some timeless truths. But I must admit to enjoying the company of those with a past time orientation. They see themselves as part of some sort of chain of being. They feel they own nothing but are simply the carers and curators of the world around them. I know that people like you *[Ed. Note: the tzadik pointed at me accusingly]* see these people's incipient conservatism and frequent aristocratic feelings of self-importance annoying. But they are not like those with timeless orientations who "aspire" to religious/spiritual/universals. These "aspirants" (as they regard themselves) assure themselves (and us) that they have acquired some sort of timeless truths. They see themselves as representatives of God/Allah/or any semantic or visual feature that they perceive as unchanging and unchangeable. Of course, anyone with even the most naïve understanding of time realizes that there is no Universe conceivable where anything is unchangeable. But on such chimeras are built entire civilizations!

You can see, as I know you are an historian, that the past orientation norms in medieval Europe were overthrown as the middle classes started to regard their capacity to change the world by planning future states (including saving and deploying capital) that characterized the industrial revolution. A shift in time orientation is the only true revolution for humans.

The explosive potential from those who adopt Present orientations seems to be behind the creativity of artists (and comedians!) as they systematically mess with our accepted notion of space and time. Often stigmatized as "revolutionary" or disturbers of the status quo, present orientated people are no threat to anyone. On the other hand, those with timeless orientation, who believe with a certainty normally born out of ignorance, tend to seek to destroy anyone who disbelieves what they assert is unquestionably true."

The tzadik paused and looked at me quizzically. He went on: "Are you following what I am saying? You asked me about time: but you cannot understand time until you grasp its function and the way that we perceive the world through its lenses. Also, you must let go of your use of clocks as a basis of understanding. Instead, it you grasp the root structures that generate alternative time orientations, then you might obtain a more profound understanding of what we might mean by time."

The tzadik stood up glaring at me at what he must have seen as an uncomprehending stare of ignorance. Furiously, he erased the sand box with his foot, and stamped off in disgust at my failings as a student or disciple.

52

THE TZADIK AND HIS HERO

I woke up yesterday thinking about the tzadik and the influence he may have had on those he encountered. But he seemed strangely isolated as if he lived in a world of his own. I wondered who he would regard as the person who had most influenced him. I assumed that it would be Einstein or some celebrated theoretician who had provided insights into the workings of the Universe. So, when I met him later that day, I decided to tax him on the subject.

"I have admired one person above all others," he said. "He was a leader who inspired me in my Socialist beliefs. He treated his people as equals and showed them that there was an ethical code they could follow which, in all likelihood, he wrote for them. He was no saint. I think he had three wives, and my suspicion is that he ended up slumming it after being born into nobility."

I was trying to imagine who this hero could be. I mentally

listed all the early Socialists I could think of Robert Owen, Charles Fourier, Pierre-Joseph Proudhon, Saint-Simon, Karl Marx, Vladimir Ilyich Lenin: but none of them seemed to fit the tzadik's description.

"Give me more of a clue and I'm sure I'll be able to guess who your hero is."

The tzadik smiled. "You were probably thinking in terms of European thinkers: but you would be a long way off. He relied on ensuring that his community had a shared set of values that largely governed how they related to one another. They never used imprisonment as a punishment. When the people ventured off into looking at alternative figureheads, he really did lose his temper. In a rage he smashed the tablets on which his rules were inscribed. The last of his rules that banned what he called covetousness confirmed his socialist principles."

"Your hero is Moses!"

"That's right."

"I didn't understand what you said about prison."

"You tell me how a community living in tents and traveling across Sinai for years was going to enforce imprisonment as a punishment."

"Do you regard him as some sort of saint?"

The tzadik laughed. "Moses was definitely not a saint. He killed an Egyptian guard. Do you know anything about his life?"

I was embarrassed that I could not remember much of what had been written in the Bible. So, the tzadik asked me to be seated and launched into a summary of his hero's life.

"I think Moses got away with quite a lot because he was born into the Pharoah's family: he may have been the revolutionary Pharaoh, Akhenaton. But murdering the guard was over the top – even for a royal prince. So, he fled to Midian. I know some commentators think this is as much a myth as the bulrush episode. But to me it rings true. The journey there was along a trade route; he was traveling alone (or, at least, not as later with tens or hundreds of thousands of Jewish refugees); it does not seem to me to be an impossibly difficult trip. What he learnt out there was to be of immense value when leading the Jews from Egypt: it was an in-depth reconnaissance. And it was in Midian where Moses met Zipporah."

I settled back into a more comfortable position so that I could better enjoy hearing something that was clearly close to the tzadik's heart. "Perhaps Moses was used to submissive women in the Egyptian courts so was ill-prepared for a relationship with someone like Zipporah. What little we know of her from Exodus reveals a powerful personality, fully able to deal with the life-and-death disputes over water that she and the women had with local shepherds. It is likely that it was the way she handled herself in such a conflict that first attracted attention. She brought Moses into her family (with her six sisters) that was dominated by the first real father he had known – Jethro. I suspect that things went wrong between him and Zipporah over quite some time. Both had strong personalities and I cannot see her as accepting the standard, female role of subservient obedience. Moses must have been awful to live with. Exiled from the Egyptian court and from the Jewish community with whom he was increasingly identifying, he must have had bouts of depression. Coming under the calm authority of Jethro and experiencing the stimulating marriage with Zipporah must have had a considerable influence. Moses' creative mind turned to plans of liberation. The seeds of what was to become the revolutionary ideology of radical monotheism – bred from Jewish and Egyptian sources and, perhaps, fertilized by his perspectives in Midian – were beginning to develop. He came home with tales of burning bush hallucinations and dialogues with God. Zipporah may have had her patience a little strained. The break appears to have come over his insistence that their son, Gershom, should be circumcised. Zipporah regarded this as a bloody and barbaric practice, but he insisted and said he would do it. She knew what a clumsy person Moses was, unused to working with his hands. So, she circumcised Gershom herself, hurled his foreskin at his father's feet, and marched out."

"Sounds a bit melodramatic to me," I interjected. The tzadik glared at me and said: "tell me, have you read Exodus recently? No? Well, you should as you'll soon learn that it is a truly dramatic story."

The tzadik took a deep breath and continued: "Moses returns to Egypt with a plan of action to liberate the Jewish community but misses Zipporah terribly. Now we come to his sister, Miriam. Again, there is precious little written evidence about her. But she is acknowledged as a prophetess. Given the extreme male chauvinism of the later redactors (no more than a reflection of the deep-rooted sexism that still pervades the area to this day), any mention of something as active and powerful as prophecy probably signifies quite an extraordinary person. Maybe Miriam was the never-to-be-mentioned power behind Moses and his younger brother, Aaron. I wonder if she organized the difficult things, the moving of the families, the feeding of the children, the community infra-structure maintained by women despite the upheaval of leaving Egypt. How much was she a leader against the oppression of Pharaoh? I do not believe that Moses would admit it even if he could. I suspect that it was she who organized the female household slaves to slip something toxic into the bedtime drink of the eldest sons of the Egyptian families on Passover night."

"Moses and the Israelites escape from Egypt with an army on their heels that gets bogged down or waterlogged – truly miraculous! The large-scale migration is big news. They hear of it out in Midian: so, Jethro tells Zipporah that Moses may be a dreamer, but the dreams look like becoming reality. A slave revolt against Pharaoh is news – a successful one is unheard of. Zipporah listens to her father: he is a justly respected elder. Moses is out in the desert, feeling even more lonely but now he has left Egypt he is nearer his wife. So, Moses sends a message and invites Jethro and the whole family to come to the celebrated encampment. They arrive. Moses is truly glad to see them and is desperate to impress his father-in-law. Above all, he really wants Zipporah back."

"What does Jethro find? Moses sitting like a judge hearing all the grievances that arise daily within the community. Such a show of authority, Moses feels, will impress Jethro and Zipporah. But at the end of the day, Jethro puts Moses in his place with words of wisdom for both him and Zipporah. He sees that the marriage will only stand a chance if both spend more time with each other. So, he tells Moses to stop his solitary ruler/judge act and just concentrate on policy. Delegate the running of the system of justice to others and think more about more important matters. One of these matters is his marriage. Moses agrees to Jethro's suggestions about how to organize the system of justice within the community: Jethro is pleased, Zipporah is happy. Jethro and his family depart back to Midian: Moses is reunited with Zipporah. Now, at last, he feels the emotional security he needs and the lifting of the organizational burden he shouldered. Now he is ready for the journey into Sinai and his enunciation of the basics of radical monotheism – the Ten Commandments."

"The Pentateuch is stuffed full of ordinances and regulations that were probably inserted into the story by later redactors to give them some legitimacy. Even some of the Commandments were probably reformulated a bit to make them sound more relevant to the post-nomadic era. But there were, no doubt, certain rules enforced as best as possible whilst Moses was in the desert. After Jethro had told him to keep off the minutiae of government, I cannot see him spending much time worrying over such details. The rituals that were part of the pomp and ceremony of the priesthood would undoubtedly have been developed by the expert in the field – Aaron. The critical hygiene laws that were the most open secret behind Jewish survival in the region for centuries to come were urgently required in those first months in the desert. I detect Miriam's work here."

"Moses' life after the giving of the Commandments is one big struggle, mainly one that he loses. We are not told, but I think Zipporah dies; maybe some of his more brutal enemies within the camp take out their vengeance against him by killing her during his absence and the Golden Calf orgies. Perhaps, in a more sinister light, it is Miriam whose nose is put out by the influence of Zipporah. When Zipporah is gone, Moses marries an Ethiopian woman, continuing the preference and the long Jewish tradition of marrying out of the community. In his youth he was probably served in every way by black slave girls whom the Arab traders would have delivered to the Egyptian court. His new marriage is perceived as regressing back to some sort of second childhood – and maybe it was. Miriam objects strongly, as does Aaron: but to no avail. Discord in the camp grows until there is a full-scale rebellion led by Korah. Its defeat costs hundreds of lives: Moses is clearly losing his grip. Marching on into an area with no water, he thinks he remembers where he can find some. He eventually arrives at the rocks where water is to be found and he strikes them, theatrically, to produce the water. But it is all too late. Miriam and Aaron, along with hundreds of others, have already died of thirst."

"Moses is no longer the leader. Without Zipporah, Miriam, and Aaron, he is regarded as no more than an ancient figure-head. Joshua is already the real commander as the wars with the indigenous communities erupt with the emergence of the nomadic Jewish tribes out of the desert. Joshua was a deft military tactician whose victories no doubt inspired Moses' final months. But I wonder how he felt as those same people who had sheltered him when a fugitive from Pharaoh, the Midianites whose families included Jethro's and Zipporah's, were slaughtered by Israeli warriors. Aaron's son, Eleazar, was now the priest and he strikes me as a nasty piece of work. Did he really order the death of every Midianite male and their wives and the enslavement of the girls? Or did Moses order it so as still to appear tough and have all his old authority? When he died soon after in Moab, I wonder to whom or to what his last thoughts were turned."

"So, you see, Moses was no saint. He was very much a man of his time. But his clarifying the basic ethical standards enforced by the most radical concept of that (or any other) time – an omnipotent, invisible, omnipresent single deity – lays the foundations of the whole of western civilization. That is why he is my hero."

After this long speech, the tzadik looked exhausted: so, I did not ask him any more about his hero. But on reflection I think I can understand why he revered this ancient figure despite all his obvious foibles and defects.

53

THE TZADIK AND DEMOCRACY

The tzadik was watching fish. I asked him if he ever tried to catch them but he shook his head. I asked him if he ever ate fish. But he shook his head.

"Why are you watching them?" I asked.

He answered with a smile: "I am looking for the fish that you never see. For those you can see are always caught but the very few you never see are never fooled by nets and rods."

I frowned and he laughed. "Surely you remember what Abraham Lincoln said? You can fool all the people some of the time, and some of the people all the time, but you cannot fool all the people all the time."

I nodded but he placed his hand on my head and said: "Unfortunately Lincoln never understood the river. For you see the truth is that there are a few fish who can never be fooled whereas you can fool most of the fish all the time."

54

THE TZADIK AND THE DAY OF JUDGEMENT

He was sitting beside the river reading a book. I had never seen the tzadik with reading material and was curious what was clearly giving him great enjoyment as he smiled and laughed as he turned the pages.

"What's the book?" I asked.

He looked up and said, "Let me read this to you. I think you'll find it amusing."

I nodded and sat beside him, and he read out loud: "I was getting bored with being dead. Now don't get me wrong, I was not being badly treated. Quite the contrary, the companion assigned to each dead person could turn out to be moody and humorless but mine was very nice. I shouted to her: "Hey, Norma; what do you do for entertainment over here?" She hovered nearby: a sweaty, out-of-breath angel, a boisterous, elephantine spirit. She flew over to me, accidentally knocking me over as she failed yet again to judge her landing. "Sorry about that," she apologized. Then she scolded me: "Now you remember your briefing when you were told that you had to be patient. You are in limbo. There is no notion of time passing for those of us who run this place. It will be better for you to learn patience, so you'll be able to forget about time too."

I glared at her. "I know all that, but meanwhile I am bored so can you tell me what I can do whilst I learn patience?" She looked uncomfortable, and I sensed she was hiding something. But she said nothing. I tried a new approach. "You say I'm in limbo, Norma. So, when can I leave this comfortable place where you look after me? When can I take important responsibilities? Is it purely when you decide I've learnt patience?"

"No, no," she cried. "It's not up to me. I'm only a companion; I'm not a voting judge!"

"What in Heaven is a voting judge?" I asked. Norma looked even more disconsolate, apologized for having mentioned the judges, and explained that she would have to get some advice on how to help me. She left worrying about whether she would be punished for having told me things I should not know. She returned in seconds. "I've been told I can take you to the judgement hall."

"Is this what I've been taught as The Last Judgement?" I asked with some trepidation. But Norma laughed and said that we all had our last judgement in the hall. "Actually," she added, "this is how you leave limbo. You have to be voted through."

We arrived at a sandy, rock-strewn hill below which was

an amphitheater with odd, echoing acoustics. A man was standing at the focal point of the great semi-circular arena declaiming to a large, noisy audience. He held a big book from which he was reading a story. As his voice rose and fell and the tale of two lovers became more twisted and impassioned, the book itself glowed with various colors. I turned to Norma and asked about the book. She smiled and explained that it was made of a divine coral that reacted to the emotion of the reader. "The voting judges amongst the spectators award points for the total performance, voice, dramatic effects and color range." The man finished his reading. As time no longer existed, I should not have been surprised when I learnt that he was a star actor who died about 1000 years after me. He was booed off the stage to return to limbo where, Norma explained, he would try to learn more about patience and brush up on his stagecraft. "What about our famous leaders?" I asked and named a few. Norma had not heard of many but became uncharacteristically vehement when I named a couple of notorious Nazis. "They can never narrate because when they hold the book, it turns black. We have to clean the pages after they have touched it. They are not given any further trials and are not returned to limbo." I did not dare ask where they were sent.

The next on the stage was Moses. He was a chubby, small man with a dreadful stammer. The story he was given to read was long and convoluted. I must admit that I lost track of it quickly, but the spectators had fallen silent astonished, I think, by the unbelievable play of light emanating from the book that projected the strangest and most evocative images around the amphitheater and onto the surrounding hillside. When he eventually finished, the audience broke into a prolonged applause. "Now, if you read like that," Norma confided, "you'll have no problem in winning over the judges." I nodded as if I understood and rose to leave. "No, don't go yet," she said. "You ought to watch the next performance, it is always so predictable." I turned back, intrigued.

There, holding the book carefully and seated cross-legged, was the Buddha. He opened the book and an expectant hush fell over the audience. I watched the book, waiting for the colors. I gazed at the great man, waiting for him to speak. But there was no play of light, and only silence. After what seemed like a long time, Buddha put the book down and left. The spectators chuckled and I turned to Norma. "What's going on?" She laughed and said, "Buddha looks down on the book, but since he has left behind all emotion, the pages are completely transparent. So, the stories written on every page appear to him as one, undifferentiated, superimposed block of characters. He can see through all of it but can read nothing. If you want to leave limbo, I wouldn't try to be like him."

55

THE TZADIK AND PLATO

Although we had never discussed philosophy or the contribution to thinking made by famous philosophers, I was curious to know what the tzadik thought about these most revered men (I could not help noticing that there were no women regarded as philosophers before the 20th century).

So, I picked up my copy of Plato's 'Republic' that I must admit I had not looked at since my school days. My recollection of its contents was scanty to say the least, but I hoped it might prove to be a spark to ignite a conversation with the tzadik.

I saw him walking towards me and he peered at the volume I deliberately held out so he could see it.

"I see you have been reading a significant treatise: have you got to the seventh book yet?"

I frowned and he could see I had no idea to what he was referring.

"You know the part where he lays out the foundations of a proper education: the curriculum of arithmetic, geometry, astronomy and music."

I could see that he was warming to the subject, and he went on: "This is what medieval thinkers called the quadrivium which was built on the trivium: grammar, logic and rhetoric. I have often spoken about the tragic demise of music as a subject. Unfortunately, latter-day educationalists believe that spending time learning how to operate information technology improves the student more."

I thought I would provoke him a little: "Surely Plato was primarily interested in the education of a governing élite. So, the subjects that he espoused were meant to lay the foundations, the concepts, and the language for that élite to use when ruling the ancient world. In China, this must have been just as the basics that Confucius expounded laid the foundations for how the Empire was to be governed. Both assume an ethical basis upon which human society can continue to exist and operate happily under the tutelage of an educated class. But nowadays people need to know how to operate modern technology. Surely you agree that chemistry and physics are more important than grammar and rhetoric?"

The tzadik smiled and shook his head. "You do not understand what you are saying. Either that or you are simply wanting to tease me. I will say nothing against the learning of scientific subjects, nor of modern languages, nor of history, nor of geography. But we are not discussing whether learning is important: we are discussing what would be the most effective basis upon which to build a curriculum. And you have said nothing against the quadrivium, nor the trivium: only those other subjects are worthy of study. But let me ask you this. If the liberal arts are meant to provide the basic understanding of the world within which we live, can you fault the teaching of mathematics as part of the curriculum?"

I shook my head as I did acknowledge maths as a fundamental subject in every curriculum, ancient and modern.

"So, if we acquire an understanding of number through arithmetic, geometry gives us that in space, music gives it to us in time and astronomy is a visual representation of how number plays out in space and time. A pretty good basis, I'm sure you agree!"

I felt I was struggling against his arguments. So, I said "I am trying to address the curriculum as an enterprise preparing everyone for the trials and tribulations of the modern world. I think you are trying to lay out a theoretical argument about the relationship between subjects which could infer which subjects were "basic" (i.e. most important) and those that somehow rested upon or deferred to the basics. We are doing different things here, aren't we?"

"Of course, but it was you who started by holding up your old, dusty copy of Plato's Republic that I do not believe you've opened in decades. You wanted to discuss education in the terms Plato laid out. All I would say to you is that modern educators are more than aware of Plato's disdain for democracy as a governing principle. They quickly dismiss much of his thinking as being in opposition to their democratic ideals. Now I would not want you to think that I agree with everything that Plato wrote. Quite the contrary, I think he was wildly off understanding many of the most significant issues that you and I have been discussing. But the arrogance of those who dismiss his thinking simply because it contrasts with theirs is usually grounded in palpable ignorance of what he wrote. There are many occasions when I feel that those in government would be more valued if they themselves valued logic, spoke with understandable grammar and used rhetoric that addressed real issues above their own. And if you want to discover where those real issues reside, you find them quickly enough if you address them in terms of the measurable quantities of what we lack (arithmetic), their relationship with the land and space around us (geometry), our feelings as we live through time (music) and the planet upon which we live (astronomy)."

I nodded in agreement and promised to re-read 'The Republic' before daring to start a discussion about Plato again.

56

THE TZADIK AND REFLECTION

I was looking down into a tiny pool that had formed beside the raging river. It was a quiet inlet from which the reflection of my face stared up from the shallow water.

"What are you doing?" the tzadik interrupted my peaceful contemplation.

"I was doing what you always do: I was meditating on the flow of the river."

"No, you were not!" he snarled. "You were looking at yourself like a narcissist."

"Surely that's little more than you do," I retorted.

"Rubbish! There is nothing more tedious than seeing yourself in reflection. I avoid such a sight whenever possible. You, on the other hand, were fondly staring at yourself."

"Surely there is much you can discern by looking intensely at yourself?"

"Like what?"

"Well, you always say that understanding the way we regard the World can explain why we see certain aspects whilst we totally miss others. So, understanding yourself can explain why we cannot understand so much."

"And you think you can do that by contemplating your reflection? What a fool you are! You can observe the World, describe what you see, and induce what sort of observer you are. You don't need to look at your own reflection. All you will see is what you think you are. Only by analyzing what you see that is NOT YOU can you discover anything of interest about yourself."

"So, when I look at you, I can discover things of interest about myself. Is that what you are saying?"

"That could be true."

"So, when you look at me, what do you discover about yourself?"

"I don't think I can say," he replied with a smile.

"Why not?"

"Verbal language has limits. There is much that is beyond its capacity to express. Why do you think the sole, universal, human mode of communication is not language – it is music."

And with that, the tzadik walked off down the towpath singing to himself.

57

THE TZADIK AND MUSIC

I had considerable misgivings about speaking with the tzadik about music. It was not so much for any reason to do with music's apparent lower status than the elevated arena within which he seemed to operate. Would he regard music as significant as quantum mechanics, general relativity or philosophy? And if he did not, how would I feel as a practicing musician and composer?

However, I was intrigued to discover his thoughts about what I regarded as the most important cultural activity. I was unsure how to broach the subject; but I should not have had any fear as he himself decided to explore the subject the next time we met.

The occasion began when I found him sitting and listening to a bird. He was very quiet and sat with an intense expression as if trying to decipher any meaning in the chirping that came from the nearby copse. After a few moments the bird flew off and I asked: "Do you think that birdsong is what inspired our early ancestors to practice what we now call music?"

The tzadik smiled and shook his head. "If music were a forest, then birdsong would be a feature of the landscape: but not its cause."

"So do you think music is like a language?"

"Many people seem to find it reassuring to categorize it like that. But you are a musician so know that such a description fails to capture much of what music is."

"So, how would you describe it?"

"Given the limitations of verbal communication, I think I would try to avoid ever having to describe music beyond the basic dictionary definition: the art of combining sounds to achieve beauty of form and expression of emotion."

"Surely we can do better than that!" I exclaimed and, knowing the tzadik's penchant for mathematics, I added: "that is like saying that pure maths is just an abstract expression of space, number and quantity."

"Well, so it is. I would not disagree with that. But what you are seeking is to better understand the significance of music to us as human beings. And as you know that music is the only cultural activity that all human societies appear to have practiced for tens of thousands of years, we can assume that it has a significance beyond anything that appears on school curricula or even beyond the economic impact of the popular music industry."

I thought about the demise of music as a subject to be studied at school. "Why do you think music is regarded so lowly by the powers that be? And why are only a tiny number of practicing musicians paid anything but a minimum amount of money?"

The tzadik grimaced. "You should look to your own history in England for at least one answer. I learnt by heart the words of your 1572 Act, "all fencers, bearwards, common players of interludes, and minstrels (not belonging to any baron of this realm, or to any other honourable person of greater degree),wandering abroad without the license of two justices at the least, were subject to be grievously whipped and burned through the gristle of the right ear with a hot iron of the compass of an inch about."

The landowners in the reign of Queen Elizabeth 1st regarded anyone not employed by themselves, the State or the Church as vagabonds and a threat to themselves. And the fact that people frequently expressed their discontentment through music and song made wandering musicians and their music a subject to be degraded and dismissed in any way that those in power were able. So, music is seen as a threat: and was still regarded as such when the Youth Culture adopted rock music. And the fascination with the Beatles and other performers caught more attention than the words of politicians and media magnates. So, those in power are always wary of the potential power of music."

"Are you saying that the meaning of music can best be discovered by uncovering the social significance that it carries?"

"Sometimes: but I suspect that music has different significance to different people as it is like a Universe in its own right. It has its own histories and traditions (both conservative and subversive), alternative notations, ways of revealing sound and silence, instrumentation, vocalizations and modes of capturing timbres, rhythms, harmonic progression and melodic improvisation. Like any form of meaningful communication, it imposes constraints within which practitioners like you are free to work and play. Outside those constraints we encounter noise as well as many of the unmediated sounds of nature, the wind, the sea, our own breathing. Within them we can express the widest possible range of emotions, thoughts and feelings."

"So do you think music is like mathematics in the purest sense?"

"Not really. There are parallels in the sense that you can operate within a parallel mathematical Universe: but their dynamics are differently structured. You will notice how music can enhance the spoken word in song whereas mathematical expression and the spoken word are uncomfortable bedfellows. I believe that the crowning glories of mathematics are where an abstraction has managed to reduce what seems like disconnected or random items into a comprehensible means of understanding. Maths is principally reductive. Music has the opposite tendency: it is essentially additive and only the imposition of the constraints the art demands prevent it from disintegrating into nothing other than a vast array of primal sound."

Then the tzadik turned to face me and asked: "Tell me, what do you think you are doing when you compose?"

I had to think about this as I sensed he wanted me to respond in a way that meant something to him. "I suspect that all I am doing is using soundscapes to manipulate the sense of duration. We are molding time just as the sculptor molds stone or clay. Does that make any sense to you?

He nodded. "I'm not sure that all music does anything to our sense of time other than falling in step with clock time. That is probably why most pop music sounds very much the same with the same structures, the same key relationships and the same rhythms."

"I sense that you are no great lover of pop music."

"I don't think that's fair. All you are saying is that pop music tends to express extremely uncomplicated emotions and that you see me as a complicated person. That does not help us better understand music: all you are doing is trying to better understand me. I thought you wanted to discuss the significance of music."

"Fair enough. But surely it is significant that certain music has a shelf life longer than a month or two whilst others are soon forgotten. The fact that we in Europe still perform the work of Bach, Mozart and Beethoven must mean that certain music is more significant than others."

"Of course: but only to certain people. Those who live much of their lives within the musical Universe – even if they are just singers on the night club circuit – are well aware of the emotional impact that can be exacted by the performance of a Beethoven symphony. Then there are the keen followers; not necessarily practicing musicians, who sense that impact and cherish the sensation. But at the two extremes you have those who describe themselves as stone deaf (I don't mean those with hearing loss) whose lives are lived entirely outside the sounds of music for whom there is little or no response to its appeal. And there are those, like you, whose lives seem to have been lived with those sounds as a permanent feature of their existence and who usually show themselves as composers and/or performers. For you and people like you there can be no escape from the sound worlds created by Beethoven, Schubert, Chopin, Mahler, Bartok ... shall I go on?"

I shook my head. I felt he had made his point: but in some way he had made it at my expense rather than providing me with some sort of objective understanding of where music fitted into the world as he saw it.

So, I began again: "Some say that music only has an impact because it refers to the society within which it has been created. This is why performance of the same work changes with the generations..."

"Yes, yes," he interrupted. "Music as an outgrowth from the social situation within which it is composed or performed is another well-worn path. But that really only tells you more about the society: it does not tell you about the music. And we know that music is often called into existence simply to amplify a certain social setting: romantic dance music bringing couples together, military music, Stalin's call for music to make Soviet citizens into happy Russians. But I think there is a more interesting area to explore although I am not well qualified to undertake it: the relationship of music to the operation and functions of the human body. Heartbeat, bipedal walking, breathing ... even laughing, coughing and crying ... all these may relate to musical practice in every culture as they are common to all human beings."

I nodded and he pointed his finger at me and shouted:

"Aha! That seems to have struck a chord with you. Perhaps that tells you more about your music."

And with a wave of his arm, he strutted off and I smiled because he was humming a tune that I had composed so he could emulate the exaggerated gait of a toy soldier.

58

THE TZADIK AND PILGRIMAGE

I did not see the tzadik for a week. I thought he might have gone off on a pilgrimage. After all, so many people who claim to be "holy" are always going on retreats where, presumably, they uncover truths about themselves. My failure to have ever attended such a place probably made me unqualified to make any judgement about their usefulness. But when I saw the tzadik the following week, I asked him where he had been.

"Nowhere in particular," he replied.

"I thought you might have gone on a pilgrimage."

The tzadik shook his head.

"Let me tell you about pilgrimages," he intoned. "There are those who, in search of fabulous wisdom, set off for far destinations – Atlantis, the Indies, Jerusalem. In pilgrimages we learn we are equal: the Haj requires the same journey and rituals no matter who we are. In our baptisms (a merging with nature), we are submerged by the same water. And on our return what do we find? The wisdom has not moved. We were equal before we set off: we were subject to the same forces of nature. And so, what drives us to make the journeys? Is it fear of standing still? Or is it incredulity at the knowledge that we already possess?"

59

THE TZADIK AND THE CANDLE

The tzadik was sitting cross-legged with his back to the river. He was staring at a single candle that he had just lit.

"What are you doing?" I asked.

He nodded his head at me and said "I'm glad you're here, I've something to tell you about this candle. Before God revealed Himself to His people, we would congregate around tribal campfires and tell each other legends. After Moses, the legends are relegated to fairy story and the fire is seen as no more than a symbol of the community – the focus for our meeting. The fire becomes the Shabbos candles lit in every home at the same moment, the story is the story of our People told every Sabbath."

"In the time of my grandmother, this was the significance of the candles. They lit the way to the Sabbath, and they were the focus for the evolving story. It was a story that we told and in which we were actors. But in the time of my mother, a change occurred – a domestication. The candles became the focus for the family rather than the whole community. We became more private: the stories were no longer told but read from books. Our parents thought of the story as fixed – they could no longer feel the pulse of it through their own veins. The candle flame became dim.

Now, in our own generation, there will come a man who will light a flame. But he will use our own books, and the teachers themselves, as torches. This will be his appeal – the return to the campfire. And folk will flock to his banner, and we shall be sacrificed. But when they come to tell stories, they will find that they do not know how. Their imagination will have long since flickered away and the conflagration that they shall cause will serve only to disguise their pale, limp spirit. So now you know why you must continue telling our story. It is a living flame; disciplined by the Sabbath; contained between the setting of the sun and lit by candles. Long after I have gone, you must keep to this true tradition – not the adherence to rigid rules, but continual improvisation, the tales of our People, the working out of our destiny in our own words."

9 781068 705700